WILLIAMS
SONOMA
CALIFORNIA

AIR FRYING WITH INSTANT POT®

ALEXIS MERSEL

PHOTOGRAPHY BY
ERIN SCOTT

weldon**owen**

CONTENTS

Spring Rolls with Nuoc Cham
(page 20)

Apricot-Ginger Glazed
Pork Chops (page 54)

FEEL-GOOD FRYING

I can't even count how many people have asked me, "Should I buy an Instant Pot® or an air fryer?" My answer was always that the Instant Pot®, which changed my life, could never be topped by another single-use device—certainly not by an air fryer! Admittedly, I was biased, having written three books focused on the Instant Pot® (*Everyday Instant Pot*, *Healthy Instant Pot*, and *Instant Pot Soups*). Then the Instant Pot Duo Crisp®—a pressure cooker and air fryer in one—changed my life again.

Whether I'm air frying homemade Chicken Nuggets (page 71) or pressure-cooking Farro (page 138) for my daughter, broiling Korean BBQ Flank Steak (page 65) for my husband, or treating myself to some Jam-Filled Brioche Doughnuts (page 117), my Instant Pot Duo Crisp® is now the most essential countertop appliance in my kitchen. I even reheat pizza and toast bread and sandwich buns in it, eliminating the need to turn on my oven and wait for it to heat up (an even bigger benefit in the summer). Not only does air frying replace deep-frying for some of my family's favorite indulgences like French fries (page 43) and chicken wings (page 30), it also broils beef and chicken to juicy perfection and bakes incredibly moist, mouthwatering cakes in less time than an oven.

With literally every cooking method at your fingertips, you can pressure cook, sauté, steam, slow cook, sous vide, air fry, bake, roast, broil, and dehydrate—just attach the pressure cooking lid or the air fryer lid, select a program, and have dinner on the table in minutes. Whether you've been using your Instant Pot® for a while and are excited to cook with the air fryer lid, or you're a novice at both pressure cooking and air frying, this book is for you. Packed with more than 80 recipes for snacks, sides, main dishes, and desserts, it shows off the versatility and health benefits of being able to "fry" a variety of foods with a fraction of the oil used in traditional frying. You'll also discover creative ways to use the high-powered convection technology to cook some unexpected dishes such as Lemon-Poppyseed Drizzle Cake, Cheese-Stuffed Beef Burgers, and Hush Puppies. You won't believe the incredible guilt-free fried flavor! As with any cooking tool, it's important to understand how the pot works before getting started (see the primer on page 8). The air frying how-tos (page 14) will help you master the technique like a pro, and a handful of essential tips and tricks (page 17) will make your life easier in the kitchen.

Trust me—air frying is not just for fries and wings. You'll be amazed at how many outstanding meals you can cook with minimal time and effort. Combining pressure cooking and air frying might just change your life, too!

Bon appétit!

INSTANT POT® PRIMER

Welcome to the new world of fast, even, and flavorful cooking. The Instant Pot Duo Crisp® and the Instant Pot Air Fryer Lid® combine the power of pressure cooking and the ease of air frying into one countertop machine.

HOW DOES IT WORK?

The Instant Pot Duo Crisp® is a pressure cooker and air fryer in one. Its 11-in-1 functionality does everything a regular Instant Pot® does, but swapping out the pressure cooking lid for the air fryer lid adds five new programs: air fry, bake, broil, roast, and dehydrate. Instead of submerging food in oil, toss or coat it with a small amount of oil (see page 14 for recommendations) to create crispy, golden brown dishes such as French fries, chicken wings, buttermilk fried chicken, fish tacos, doughnuts, and churros. The machine also cooks a variety of foods that are not typically fried but benefit from high heat and rapid air circulation, such as ribs, marinated steak, corn on the cob, brussels sprouts, pork chops, and fish. The stand-alone Instant Pot Air Fryer Lid® transforms your regular 6-quart (6-L) Instant Pot® into a powerful air fryer with the same functionality of the Duo Crisp. Both the Duo Crisp and the Air Fryer Lid can be used to create the recipes in this book.

When pressure cooking, the tightly sealed pot boils liquid quickly, then traps the steam and generates pressure. With this method, heat is evenly, deeply, and quickly distributed. The Duo Crisp features two pressure levels: Lo is best for fish, seafood, eggs, and soft vegetables, while Hi is most effective for meat, poultry, root and other hard vegetables, grains, beans, oats, chili, stock, and broth.

Like pressure cooking, air frying helps you save time and cook healthy meals—without using a lot of energy or heating up your kitchen. The air fryer lid relies on the Instant Pot® proprietary EvenCrisp technology to produce tender, juicy dishes with a crisp, golden finish with little or no oil. It relies on very hot, fast-blowing air to cook and crisp food, similar to the way a convection oven works. You can use it to cook food from fresh or frozen, or to crisp up a dish after it's been cooked on a pressure-cooking setting. Compared to a full-size oven, the Air Fryer Lid is also a fast, easy, and energy-efficient way to reheat and recrisp leftovers.

PARTS & ACCESSORIES

The Instant Pot Air Fryer Lid® attaches to your existing Instant Pot® and is compatible with the following models: Duo 60, Duo Plus 60, Ultra 60, Viva 60, Nova Plus 60, and Duo Nova 60. Each model has slightly different features, with more than a dozen distinct cooking programs from which to choose, depending on the model. Using the pressure cooking lid, you can sauté, sear, steam, simmer, slow cook, pressure cook, and braise in the machine, while the air fryer lid lets you air fry, broil, bake, roast, and dehydrate. Only use the air fryer lid with stainless-steel inner pots, not ceramic inner pots.

Pressure Cooking Lid: Allows you to sauté, pressure cook, slow cook, steam, sous vide, delay start, and keep food warm. These programs do not air fry.

Air Fryer Lid: Allows you to air fry, roast, bake, broil, and dehydrate.

The Duo Crisp and the Air Fryer Lid come with a variety of accessories designed for use with the machine's air fry programs.

Multilevel air fryer basket and base: Fits inside the inner pot to hold the majority of your foods for air frying, broiling, and roasting.

Dehydrating tray: Also referred to as a broiling tray; fits inside the air fryer basket to bring foods closer to the heating element, which is helpful for melting cheese, toasting buns, and crisping taquitos.

Multifunctional rack: Fits inside the inner pot and is used to steam or bake foods.

Protective pad and storage cover: Stores the lid safely after frying and when not in use.

All oven-safe cookware is safe to use in the inner pot. The multifunctional rack will ensure your food is steamed and not boiled by providing even heat distribution and preventing food from scorching on the bottom of the pot.

The cooker base handles are equipped with a rectangular slot where you can store the pressure cooking lid when not in use. You can keep your counters dry and save space by inserting the left or right lid fin of the pressure cooking lid into the corresponding slot on the cooker base. Once the lid is safely in the standing position, it's easy to remove the inner pot.

FUNCTIONS & SETTINGS

Both lids correspond to their own set of smart programs. With the pressure cooking lid, you can use the smart programs to sauté, pressure cook, slow cook, steam, and sous vide. With the air fryer lid, you can air fry, roast, bake, broil, and dehydrate.

Pressure cooking uses steam pressure to raise the boiling point of water above 212°F (100°C). This energy-efficient method is a fast and easy way to thoroughly and evenly cook a variety of your favorite meals. The Pressure Cook and Steam smart programs are pressure cooking programs.

Sauté: This function allows you to sear meat before pressure cooking or after sous vide cooking, simmer stock, reduce liquid, and more, similar to how you use a sauté pan on the stovetop. It has three modes: Less is ideal for cooking bacon or other foods that might stick; Normal is best for simmering, thickening, and reducing liquids; and More is handy for browning meat. The timer on this function is automatically set for 30 minutes, but in the rare case when you might need it on for longer than that, just press the Sauté button again after it shuts off and continue cooking. Never put the locking lid on while using this function.

Pressure Cook: There are two levels for pressure cooking, Hi and Lo. Most recipes call for the Hi setting. The Lo setting can be used for delicate foods like fish or eggs. Press the Pressure Level key or Adjust key (depending on your model) to adjust pressure levels, and the + and - keys to change the cooking time.

Slow Cook: This is a non–pressure cooking program, where the Less, Normal, and High modes correspond to the low, medium, and high settings of some temperature-controlled slow cookers. It works similarly to a traditional slow cooker, cooking food very, very slowly with more liquid than required for pressure cooking. You can use this function for preparing your favorite slow-cooker recipes.

Steam: For this program, always use the steam rack that came with the pot or a metal or silicone steam basket. The pot comes to pressure on full, continuous heat, and the food can scorch if it's not raised off the bottom of the pot.

Sous Vide: Sous vide cooking brings vacuum-sealed food to a very accurate temperature and maintains that temperature for a long period of time to achieve high-quality, consistently delicious results. To use this program, you'll need tongs, an instant-read thermometer, and airtight or vacuum-sealed food pouches. Refer to the pot's manual for specific sous vide cooking guidelines.

Keep Warm/Cancel: These buttons, sometimes combined into one, turn off any cooking program so that you can switch to another program or end the cooking. The Keep Warm setting holds the food at a safe temperature for up to 10 hours.

Delay Start: This feature allows you to delay the start of cooking, which is particularly handy if you want to soak dried beans before cooking them. Delay Start may be applied to the Pressure Cook, Slow Cook, and Steam smart programs. To set a Delay Start timer, select a smart program and adjust the settings as you like, then press Delay Start. You can set Delay Start for a minimum of 10 minutes to a maximum of 24 hours.

Time Display: The countdown timer indicates cooking and Delay Start time in hours and minutes (05:20 is 5 hours, 20 minutes). The timer counts up while in Keep Warm.

Temperature/Pressure Display: The pressure cooking lid display indicates Lo (Low) or Hi (High) pressure or temperature level. When using the sous vide smart program, the display specifies temperature in °F (Fahrenheit) or °C (Celsius). The air fryer lid display indicates temperature in °F or °C.

PRESSURE RELEASE

On most 6-quart (6-L) models compatible with the air fryer lid, the steam release valve has two positions—Venting and Sealing. The pot can come up to pressure only when the lid is locked and the valve is set to Sealing. On the Duo Crisp,

the steam release value is automatically set to sealing. As a safety precaution, you will not be able to open the lid unless the valve is switched to Venting (on the 6-quart/6-L models) or the Quick Release Button is pressed (on the Duo Crisp).

There are two main ways to release the pressure when the program ends:

Quick Release: Manually turn the valve to Venting or press the Quick Release Button as soon as the cooking program has ended. Take care when moving the valve: use an oven mitt, wooden spoon, or kitchen tongs instead of bare hands, and do not put your face over or near the valve since the steam will shoot out quickly.

Natural Release: The pot will lose pressure on its own as it cools. The time needed for a natural pressure release varies depending on the volume of food and liquid in the pot (the greater the amount, the longer it will take) and can be as quick as a few minutes or up to 30 minutes. Once the program has finished, the pot defaults to the Keep Warm setting and will remain there for up to 10 hours.

You can also perform a combination of the two releases, letting the pressure release naturally for a few minutes and then turning the valve to Venting or pressing the Quick Release Button to quick-release any residual steam.

PRESSURE COOKING PRACTICALITIES

- Unlike a slow cooker, which allows liquids to evaporate and reduce during cooking, a pressure cooker is completely sealed and therefore loses no steam during cooking. To come up to pressure, the pot needs enough steam buildup, which is created from the amount of liquid in the recipe.

- Be sure to respect the fill line: to leave room for the steam buildup, the inner pot should never be more than two-thirds full.

- The steam release valve might feel a bit wobbly when switching between Venting and Sealing.

- The program timer will not start until the machine has come up to pressure.

- All of the pressure needs to be released before you can remove the lid from the pot.

AIR FRYING PROGRAMS

Air Fry: The most common air frying program, this setting produces food with a crispy exterior, such as French fries, chicken wings, potatoes, breaded cutlets, meatballs, fish and seafood, tofu, doughnuts, fritters, and more.

Roast: The Roast setting is best for large cuts of meat.

Broil: Using direct, top-down heating, Broil yields extremely juicy chicken and beef dishes. You can place foods for broiling either in the air fryer basket or on the broil/dehydrating tray, which brings them closer to the pot's heating element.

Bake: This setting is ideal for cakes, quick breads, brownies, and cookies. If baking in the multilevel air fryer basket, line the interior with parchment paper for recipes involving loose batter. (You can also purchase air fryer liners, which have tiny holes to help the air circulate.) If using a baking dish, place the rack on the bottom of the inner pot, then place the dish on the rack in the inner pot. Leave about 1 inch (2.5 cm) of space around all sides of the dish to allow heat to circulate evenly.

Dehydrate: This program applies low heat over a long period of time to safely dry out foods. Use it for preparing fruit leather, jerky, and dried fruits and vegetables.

CLEANING

Before the first use, remove the inner pot from the cooker base and wash it with hot water and dish soap. The inner pot is also dishwasher safe. Wash the accessories with hot water and dish soap, then rinse with warm water and dry with a soft cloth.

After each use, wash accessories and parts with hot water and mild dish soap and then air dry, or place on the top rack of the dishwasher. Never clean them with harsh detergents, powders, or scouring pads.

You can coat the air fryer basket and/or dehydrating tray with nonstick cooking spray before adding food for easier cleanup.

- Store the sealing ring in a well-ventilated area to decrease any residual odor. To eliminate odors, add 1 cup (240 ml) water and 1 cup (240 ml) white vinegar to the inner pot and run the Pressure Cook program for 5–10 minutes, then quick-release the pressure. You can also use one sealing ring for sweet dishes and one for savory.

- To remove baked-on grease and food residue from accessories and the air fryer lid, spray them with a mixture of baking soda and white vinegar and wipe clean with a damp cloth. For stubborn stains, let the mixture sit on the affected area for several minutes before scrubbing clean.

Inner pot: Wash the inner pot after each use and be sure that all of the outside surfaces are dry before placing it in the cooker base. To remove hard water staining, dampen a sponge with white vinegar and scrub gently. If there is tough or burned food residue at the bottom, soak the pot in hot water for a few hours before cleaning.

Air fryer lid: Let the air fryer lid cool to room temperature, then clean the heating element and surrounding area with a damp soft cloth or sponge. Wipe the exterior clean with a damp soft cloth or sponge.

Cooker base: Clean the cooker base and control panel with a barely damp soft cloth or sponge. Do not rinse or immerse the cooker base in water.

An air fryer and pressure cooker in one, the Instant Pot Duo Crisp® makes easy work of preparing dishes that typically require many steps or long cooking times. A combination of pressure cooking and broiling produces exceptionally juicy and crispy results for Asian-Style Pork Ribs (page 57) and Salt & Pepper Whole Roast Chicken (page 75).

AIR FRYING HOW-TOS

The recipes in this book teach you how to "fry" a variety of favorite foods with a fraction of the oil used in traditional frying and offer creative ways for using the high-powered convection technology to cook a selection of unexpected dishes. These guidelines will help you master air frying in no time.

The Instant Pot Duo Crisp + Air Fryer® all-in-one machine and the stand-alone Instant Pot Air Fryer Lid® use rapid air circulation to crisp or cook food, giving your meals all the rich, crispy flavor of deep-frying, with little or no oil. There are a couple of ways to use the air fryer lid:

- Give your dish a crunchy, golden finish after cooking with the Pressure Cook, Slow Cook, Steam, or Sous Vide smart programs.

- Cook your dish entirely using the air fryer lid with the Air Fry, Roast, Bake, or Broil smart programs.

- You can fit a lot of ingredients in the inner pot, but for best results, give the food room to breathe and don't overcrowd. For most recipes, place the ingredients in a single layer in the air fryer basket, making sure there is space for the hot air to circulate. If everything doesn't fit in one layer, cook in batches, as for chicken cutlets and meatballs.

- Some baked recipes call for a ceramic dish or baking pan set on the steam rack instead of in the air fryer basket. Any oven-safe cookware can be used in the inner pot.

- After lifting the air fryer lid off the cooker base, always place it on the protection pad provided. Do not rest the lid on a countertop or on its power cord. To store your air fryer lid, flip the protective pad over so the grooved side faces up. Align the back of the air fryer lid with OPEN on the protective pad, then turn the air fryer lid clockwise to the lock position.

- Depending on the smart program, the air fryer lid may beep partway through to remind you to turn the food. If you don't lift the lid, the air fryer will continue cooking at the selected temperature until the designated time is up. The recipes in this book indicate whether you should flip or rotate the food or cook it undisturbed.

- An air fryer works similarly to a powerful convection oven. To adapt an existing recipe from a conventional oven, a rule of thumb is to decrease the temperature by 25°F (-4°C) and reduce the cooking time by 25 percent.

- It's a good idea to invest in an instant-read meat thermometer to ensure food is cooked safely and doesn't dry out. Since cuts of meat can be different sizes and thicknesses, a thermometer is the only way to guarantee it is cooked correctly and not overdone.

TYPES OF OIL

Cooking oil sprays are available in many types, including canola, vegetable, olive, coconut, and avocado oil. The most commonly used sprays in this book are canola and olive oil. Just as with other cooking methods, these oils stand up well to high temperatures. Opt for canola oil spray when you want a neutral-flavored oil to blend in with food and use olive oil to enhance the flavors. You can use store-bought oil sprays or make your own with a spray bottle or aerosol mister. Unless otherwise noted in a recipe, be generous with oil sprays. The oil acts as a barrier between the fast-circulating hot air and your food, so it not only helps to create a golden brown color and crispy texture on the outside, but also keeps food moist inside.

Fried Banana Egg Rolls
(page 120)

TIPS & TRICKS

Once you're familiar with the basics of your machine, the fun begins. Don't worry about feeling like a novice—the more you use the air fryer, the more comfortable you'll become, and the more you'll be able to customize recipes and cooking times to your preference.

- Many recipes in this book use breading to create a crispy exterior while insulating the food inside from direct contact with high heat. When breading food, it's helpful to use one hand for wet steps, such as eggs and batters, and the other hand for the dry steps, such as flour and bread crumbs.

- Large, rimmed baking sheets (also known as sheet trays) are great for cooking prep and hold quite a bit more food than a standard plate. Line them with parchment paper for easy cleanup.

- A small range of ingredients can produce a variety of flavor profiles. To cook a host of dishes any night of the week, keep some staples on hand in the fridge and pantry, including garlic, ginger, green onions, lemons, limes, toasted sesame oil, soy sauce, rice vinegar, fish sauce, brown sugar, and honey.

- Let meat rest after cooking so the juices have a chance to redistribute, making the meat juicier and tastier. Let steaks and chops rest for 5–10 minutes and roasts for 15–20. The meat will continue to cook after it's removed from the heat, adding anywhere from 5–10°F to the internal temperature, so an instant-read thermometer is key to avoiding overcooked meat.

- The air fryer is handy for reheating leftovers, whether or not they were originally cooked in the air fryer. While reheating time and temperature will vary, start by setting the cook time for 5 minutes at 350°F (180°C) and add more time as needed.

- When air frying, later batches will be slightly darker in color due to the residual heat of the pot. If you're cooking many batches, reduce the cooking time of subsequent batches by 1 or 2 minutes to prevent overcooking or burning.

TOOLS OF THE TRADE

A few key tools are essential to preparing a selection of recipes in this book. They include:

 7-inch (18-cm) cake pan or springform pan for baking brownies and cookies

 1½-quart (1.5-L) round oven-safe baking dish for frittatas and bread pudding

 8-inch (20-cm) Bundt pan for banana bread and cakes

 Kitchen tongs for browning meat and for transferring food from the pot and air fryer basket to a plate

 Instant-read thermometer for checking the temperature of meat and fish

Crispy Brussels Sprouts with
Honey-Lime Glaze (page 41)

SNACKS & SIDES

Spring Rolls with Nuoc Cham

A sweet, sour, salty, savory, and spicy dipping sauce, nuoc cham is the perfect partner for crispy spring rolls filled with a rich blend of ground pork, shiitake mushrooms, cabbage, and carrots. Experiment with the filling ingredients to suit your taste, but be sure to remove any excess moisture with paper towels so the wrappers won't get soggy. Purchase frozen spring roll wrappers made with wheat, not the rice wrappers used for summer rolls and fresh spring rolls.

SERVES 4

Select Sauté on the Instant Pot®, press Start, and heat the oil. Add the shallot, garlic, and ¼ teaspoon pepper and cook, stirring occasionally, until fragrant, about 1 minute. Add the ground pork and 1 teaspoon of the soy sauce and cook, breaking up the meat with a wooden spoon and stirring occasionally, until the pork has started to release some fat, 2–3 minutes. Add the cabbage, carrots, mushrooms, fish sauce, sugar, the remaining 2 teaspoons soy sauce, and ½ teaspoon salt and cook, stirring occasionally, until the cabbage has wilted and the pork is cooked through, 3–4 minutes. Press the Cancel button to reset the program.

Transfer the pork mixture to a paper towel–lined plate. Wipe out or rinse the pot.

Fill a small bowl with cool water. Working with 1 spring roll wrapper at a time, place it on a work surface positioned in a diamond shape (cover the other wrappers with a damp cloth so they won't dry out). Spread ¼ cup of the pork filling in a horizontal line on the lower third of the wrapper, leaving at least a ½-inch (12-mm) border around the filling. Dip your finger in the bowl of water and moisten the edges of the wrapper. Fold the bottom corner over the filling, encasing it. Fold in the left and right corners toward the center and roll the wrapper away from you into a tight cylinder. Transfer to a plate. Repeat with the remaining wrappers and filling.

1 tablespoon canola oil

1 shallot, minced

2 cloves garlic, minced

Kosher salt and freshly ground black pepper

½ lb (225 g) ground pork

1 tablespoon soy sauce

1½ cups (4½ oz/130 g) chopped napa cabbage

½ cup (1¾ oz/50 g) shredded carrots

2 oz (60 g) fresh shiitake mushrooms or rehydrated dried shiitake mushrooms, stemmed and caps diced

2 teaspoons fish sauce

2 teaspoons sugar

10 (8-inch/20-cm) square frozen spring roll wrappers, made with wheat flour, thawed

2 tablespoons toasted sesame oil

continued from page 20

Insert the air fryer basket into the Instant Pot®. Working in batches, brush the spring rolls generously with the sesame oil and arrange a single layer of rolls in the Instant Pot® air fryer basket, making sure they don't touch. Insert the basket into the pot and attach the air fryer lid. Press the Air Fry button and set the cook time for 8 minutes at 400°F (200°C), then press Start. Cook undisturbed.

Meanwhile, make the nuoc cham: In a small bowl, stir together the warm water, lime juice, sugar, and vinegar. Add the fish sauce, chiles, and garlic and stir to combine. Taste and adjust the seasoning with lime juice and sugar if needed.

When the cooking time is up, the spring rolls should be light golden brown and slightly darker golden brown on the ends. If a darker color is desired, cook for 2 minutes longer. Use tongs to carefully transfer the spring rolls to a plate. Repeat to cook the remaining batches. Serve with the nuoc cham alongside for dipping.

FOR THE NUOC CHAM

½ cup (120 ml) warm water

3 tablespoons fresh lime juice, plus more as needed

2 tablespoons sugar, plus more as needed

2 teaspoons rice vinegar

3 tablespoons fish sauce

1 or 2 red Thai or small serrano chiles, seeded, if desired, and thinly sliced

1 clove garlic, minced

Buffalo Cauliflower Bites

An excellent vegetarian option for game days, cauliflower can stand up to high heat and hot sauce just as well as chicken. Cut florets into similar sizes so they cook evenly, and leave a flat surface on one side to help the egg mixture and breading adhere. Because hot sauce stains, it's best to use stainless-steel or glass bowls for this recipe.

SERVES 4–6

In a large bowl, whisk together the ketchup, hot pepper sauce, egg whites, 1 teaspoon salt, and ¼ teaspoon black pepper. Place the bread crumbs in a medium bowl or on a large plate.

Line a rimmed baking sheet with parchment paper. Working in batches, toss the cauliflower florets in the ketchup mixture to coat. Transfer to the bread crumbs and toss to coat completely. Place the coated cauliflower on the prepared baking sheet as you go. Repeat to coat the remaining florets.

Coat the Instant Pot® air fryer basket with canola oil spray. Working in batches, spray the cauliflower florets with oil spray and arrange a single layer of florets in the basket, making sure they touch as little as possible. Insert the basket into the pot and attach the air fryer lid. Press the Air Fry button and set the cook time for 20 minutes at 325°F (165°C), then press Start. Gently toss the cauliflower when prompted, then coat the cauliflower again.

When the cooking time is up, use tongs to carefully transfer the cauliflower to a bowl, or remove the basket from the pot and carefully pour the cauliflower into a bowl. Repeat to cook the remaining batches. Serve hot with blue cheese dip alongside.

¼ cup (2 oz/60 g) ketchup

¼ cup (60 ml) hot pepper sauce, such as Frank's RedHot cayenne pepper sauce

2 large egg whites

Kosher salt and freshly ground black pepper

2 cups (7 oz/200 g) panko bread crumbs

1 head cauliflower, cut into large florets

Blue Cheese Dip (page 33), for serving

Mozzarella Sticks with Marinara Sauce

This simple recipe has three crucial steps—double-dipping the sticks in egg and bread crumbs, freezing the sticks before frying, and cooking for exactly 4 minutes (any longer and the cheese will ooze out into a gooey mess). Resist the urge to dig right in—letting the sticks rest for 1 minute allows the heat from the breading to transfer into the cheese, creating a delightful stringy center.

SERVES 4

To cut the block of cheese, using a sharp knife, slice into rectangles about 3 inches (7.5 cm) long, 1 inch (2.5 cm) wide, and ½ inch (12 mm) thick. If using mozzarella sticks, cut the sticks in half horizontally.

In a medium bowl, whisk together the eggs and water. In a large bowl or on a plate, stir together the bread crumbs, Parmesan, and ½ teaspoon salt.

Line a rimmed baking sheet with parchment paper. Working with a few sticks at a time, dip the mozzarella in the egg mixture, letting the excess drip off, then dredge in the bread crumb mixture, turning to coat well and pressing gently to adhere. Dip the mozzarella in the egg mixture again, then dredge again in the bread crumbs. Place the coated mozzarella on the prepared baking sheet as you go. Cover the baking sheet tightly with plastic wrap and freeze for at least 2 hours or up to 2 days.

Coat the Instant Pot® air fryer basket with canola oil spray. Working in batches, coat the mozzarella sticks generously with olive oil spray and arrange a single layer of sticks in the basket, making sure they don't touch. Return the remaining mozzarella to the freezer. Insert the basket into the pot and attach the air fryer lid. Press the Air Fry button and set the cook time for 4 minutes at 375°F (190°C), then press Start. Cook undisturbed.

When the cooking time is up, use tongs to carefully transfer the mozzarella sticks to a plate (the cheese will be very soft). Sprinkle with Parmesan and let rest for at least 1 minute. Repeat to cook the remaining batches. Serve with marinara sauce alongside for dipping.

2 large eggs

1 tablespoon water

¾ cup (2½ oz/75 g) dried plain or Italian bread crumbs

2 tablespoons freshly grated Parmesan cheese, plus more for serving

Kosher salt

1 block (½ lb/225 g) mozzarella cheese, preferably whole milk, or 8 mozzarella sticks

Marinara Sauce (page 135), for serving

Cheesy Arancini

What could possibly be better than creamy risotto? Risotto that's shaped into balls, filled with cheese, and then fried. This classic Italian appetizer is much easier

SERVES 4–6

Select Sauté on the Instant Pot®, press Start, and heat the oil. Add the onion and garlic and cook, stirring occasionally, until softened, about 3 minutes. Add the rice and cook, stirring occasionally, until translucent with a white dot in the center, about 3 minutes. Add the wine and bring to a simmer, stirring occasionally with a wooden spoon to scrape up any browned bits. Cook until the wine has reduced almost completely, then stir in the stock. Press the Cancel button to reset the program.

Lock the pressure-cooking lid in place and turn the valve to Sealing. Press the Pressure Cook button and set the cook time for 7 minutes at high pressure, then press Start.

When the cooking time is up, let the steam release naturally for at least 15 minutes, then press the Quick Release Button or turn the valve to Venting to quick-release any residual steam. Carefully remove the lid.

Stir in the Parmesan, butter, ¾ teaspoon salt, and a few grindings of pepper. Transfer the risotto to a rimmed baking sheet and use a rubber spatula to spread in an even layer. Cover tightly with plastic wrap, pressing it directly on the rice, and refrigerate for at least 2 hours or up to 2 days. The risotto will be sticky.

Line another rimmed baking sheet with parchment paper. Scoop a heaping 2 tablespoons of the risotto into your palm and roll it into a ball about 2 inches (5 cm) in diameter, or use a large ice cream scoop about 2¼ inches (6 cm) in diameter. Using your fingertip, press down on the center of the ball to make a pocket about ½ inch (12 mm) deep. Place a pinch of mozzarella in the pocket, then reshape the ball to enclose the filling. (If the balls start to stick to your hands, moisten your hands with cool water.) Place the balls on the prepared baking sheet as you go.

2 tablespoons olive oil

1 yellow onion, diced

2 cloves garlic, minced

2 cups (14 oz/400 g) Arborio rice

½ cup (120 ml) white wine

4 cups (950 ml) vegetable or chicken stock (page 130 or store-bought)

½ cup (2 oz/60 g) freshly grated Parmesan cheese, plus more for serving

1 tablespoon unsalted butter

Kosher salt and freshly ground black pepper

1 cup (4 oz/115 g) shredded mozzarella cheese

and healthier when cooked using a combo pressure cooker/air fryer method. Enjoy on their own or serve with marinara sauce for dipping.

Place the flour in a medium bowl. In a shallow bowl, whisk together the eggs and milk. In another medium bowl or on a large plate, stir together the bread crumbs, oregano, 1 teaspoon salt, and ½ teaspoon pepper.

Working with 1 ball at a time, coat each in flour, shaking off the excess. Dip in the egg mixture, allowing the excess to drip off. Dredge in the bread crumb mixture, turning to coat well and pressing well to adhere. Place the coated balls back on the baking sheet as you work.

Coat the Instant Pot® air fryer basket with canola oil spray. Working in batches, coat the arancini generously with olive oil spray and arrange a single layer of balls in the basket, making sure they don't touch. Insert the basket into the pot and attach the air fryer lid. Press the Air Fry button and set the cook time for 14 minutes at 400°F (200°C), then press Start. Rotate the balls when prompted, coating both sides again with olive oil spray.

When the cooking time is up, use tongs to carefully transfer the arancini to a plate. Repeat to cook the remaining batches. Sprinkle with Parmesan and serve with marinara sauce alongside for dipping.

NOTE *The coated arancini can be frozen for up to 3 months before cooking. Freeze the balls in a single layer on a rimmed baking sheet for at least 2 hours, then transfer to a large lock-top plastic bag or freezer-safe container. Thaw in the refrigerator completely before cooking.*

¼ **cup (1 oz/30 g) all-purpose flour**

2 large eggs

2 tablespoons whole milk

1 cup (3½ oz/100 g) plain dried bread crumbs

1 teaspoon dried oregano

Marinara Sauce (page 135), for serving

Hush Puppies

These bite-size treats made from cornmeal batter are right at home alongside your favorite fried seafood. They're best eaten fresh from the fryer, so prepare these last on your menu—you can mix the batter a few hours ahead and refrigerate until ready to use.

MAKES ABOUT 18

In a medium bowl, whisk together the cornmeal, flour, sugar, baking powder, 1½ teaspoons salt, and the cayenne (if using). In a small bowl or glass measuring cup, whisk together the buttermilk, egg, and green onion. Add the buttermilk mixture to the cornmeal mixture and stir with a rubber spatula until combined. Fold in the corn.

Line the Instant Pot® air fryer basket with an air fryer liner or parchment paper cut to fit. Working in batches, use a small ice cream scoop about 1½ inches (4 cm) in diameter or a tablespoon measure to drop the batter onto the liner or parchment, leaving about ½ inch (12 mm) between the rounds. Coat them generously with canola oil spray. Insert the basket into the pot and attach the air fryer lid. Press the Air Fry button and set the cook time for 9 minutes at 400°F (200°C), then press Start. Coat the rounds again with oil when prompted to flip, but don't flip them.

When the cooking time is up, use tongs to carefully transfer the hush puppies to a plate. Repeat to cook the remaining batches, then serve.

1 cup (4½ oz/130 g) cornmeal

¾ cup (3 oz/90 g) all-purpose flour

1 tablespoon sugar

1½ teaspoons baking powder

Kosher salt

Pinch of cayenne pepper (optional)

1 cup (240 ml) full-fat buttermilk or ¾ cup (180 ml) low-fat buttermilk

1 large egg

1 green onion, white parts and pale green parts, finely chopped

½ cup (3 oz/90 g) fresh corn kernels (from about 1 ear) or frozen corn kernels

Crab Rangoon

If fresh wonton wrappers aren't available for this retro appetizer, you can find them frozen in the freezer section of Asian markets or large grocery stores— just be sure to thaw the wrappers before working with them.

SERVES 4

In a medium bowl, stir together the crabmeat, cream cheese, green onions, and Worcestershire sauce.

Line a rimmed baking sheet with parchment paper. Fill a small bowl with cool water. Working with 1 wonton wrapper at a time, place it on a work surface. Place a heaping 1 teaspoon of the crab filling in the center of the wrapper. Dip your finger in the bowl of water and moisten the edges of the wrapper. Bring the opposite corners of the wrapper up to meet each other and gently pinch them together. Bring the two remaining corners of the wrapper up to meet the other corners and gently pinch all four corners together, removing any air pockets, and seal the wrapper into an X shape. Transfer to the prepared baking sheet. Repeat with the remaining wrappers and filling.

Working in batches, coat the wontons on all sides with canola oil spray and arrange a single layer of wontons in the Instant Pot® air fryer basket, making sure they don't touch. Insert the basket into the pot and attach the air fryer lid. Press the Air Fry button and set the cook time for 8 minutes at 340°F (171°C), then press Start. Cook undisturbed.

When the cooking time is up, if the wontons are not golden brown and crisp, add more cooking time in 2-minute intervals until wontons are cooked to desired crispness. Use tongs to carefully transfer the wontons to a plate. Repeat to cook the remaining batches. Serve with chili sauce or duck sauce alongside for dipping.

NOTE *Wonton wrappers made with egg work best for this recipe. If using wrappers not made with egg, add more cooking time, if needed, until the wontons are golden and crisp. The top edges will be slightly darker than the rest of the wontons. If using very thin egg wrappers, use ½ teaspoon filling per wrapper and cook at 300°F (150°C) for 10–12 minutes.*

3 oz (90 g) cooked crabmeat, preferably lump

2 oz (60 g) cream cheese, at room temperature

2 tablespoons chopped green onions, white and pale green parts

1½ teaspoons Worcestershire sauce

16 square wonton wrappers, preferably made with egg (see note)

Thai sweet chili sauce or duck sauce, for serving

Wings Four Ways

Air frying chicken wings couldn't be easier, no matter what flavor sauce is your favorite. Simply coat the wings with a little canola oil and air fry, then toss the warm wings with the sauce after cooking. Make a few batches for your next party so you can try all of the sauces featured here.

SERVES 4-6

In a large bowl, toss together the chicken wings and oil.

Coat the Instant Pot® air fryer basket with canola oil spray and add the wings, stacking them to leave as much space as possible between them. Insert the basket into the pot and attach the air fryer lid. Press the Air Fry button and set the cook time for 25 minutes at 400°F (200°C), then press Start. Rotate and flip the wings when prompted.

Meanwhile, make the sauce(s) of your choice. (Sauce measurements will cover a full 2-pound recipe of wings. If using multiple sauces for one batch of wings, you'll only need to use a portion of each sauce, not the full amount.)

When the cooking time is up, use tongs to carefully transfer the wings to a clean large bowl. Toss the wings with the sauce to coat well. If using multiple sauces, divide the wings among multiple bowls and toss the desired amount of sauce with each bowl of wings. (If making BBQ wings, use only as much sauce as needed, ½–1 cup (120–240 ml), depending on the desired texture.) Serve right away.

2 lb (1 kg) chicken wings

1 tablespoon canola oil

Sauces of choice (recipes follow)

SESAME SAUCE

In a small saucepan over medium heat, stir together the soy sauce, hoisin sauce, sesame oil, honey, vinegar, and garlic. Bring to a gentle simmer and cook, stirring occasionally, until the sauce is reduced by one-fourth, about 8 minutes. If the sauce begins to simmer too vigorously, reduce the heat to medium-low. Remove from the heat. After coating the wings with the sauce, sprinkle with the green onions and sesame seeds.

3 tablespoons soy sauce

3 tablespoons hoisin sauce

3 tablespoons toasted sesame oil

3 tablespoons honey

1 tablespoon rice vinegar

1 clove garlic, grated

2 green onions, white and pale green parts, thinly sliced

1 tablespoon toasted sesame seeds

SPICY HONEY SAUCE

In a small saucepan over medium heat, stir together the honey, Sriracha, soy sauce, butter, and lime juice. Bring to a boil, then reduce the heat to medium-low and simmer until the sauce has thickened slightly, 2–3 minutes. Remove from the heat.

½ cup (6 oz/170 g) honey

¼ cup (60 ml) Sriracha or other hot sauce

3 tablespoons soy sauce

2 tablespoons unsalted butter

Juice of 1 lime

BUFFALO SAUCE

In a small saucepan over medium heat, melt the butter. Add the garlic and cook, stirring frequently, until fragrant, about 2 minutes. Add the hot pepper sauce and vinegar and stir to combine. Remove from the heat. After coating the wings with the sauce, serve the blue cheese dip alongside (recipe follows).

4 tablespoons (2 oz/60 g) unsalted butter

3 cloves garlic, minced

¼ cup (60 ml) hot pepper sauce, such as Frank's RedHot cayenne pepper sauce

1 teaspoon distilled white vinegar

BLUE CHEESE DIP

In a small bowl, stir together the sour cream, blue cheese, garlic, ¼ teaspoon salt, and a few grindings of pepper. Taste and adjust the seasoning with salt and pepper.

1 cup (8 oz/225 g) sour cream

½ cup (2½ oz/70 g) crumbled blue cheese

2 cloves garlic, minced or grated

Kosher salt and freshly ground black pepper

Blistered Shishito Peppers

When shishito peppers are in season, there's no simpler or better starter to a meal than peppers seared in hot olive oil and sprinkled with salt. Now this summer treat is even easier, with no frying pan required. If you're feeding a crowd, cook in batches of about ½ lb (225 g) peppers at a time so they'll have enough room in the basket to blister.

SERVES 2

In a bowl, toss together the shishito peppers, oil, and ¼ teaspoon kosher salt.

Coat the Instant Pot® air fryer basket with canola oil spray and add the peppers. Insert the basket into the pot and attach the air fryer lid. Press the Air Fry button and set the cook time for 6 minutes at 400°F (200°C), then press Start. Toss the peppers when prompted.

When the cooking time is up, use tongs to carefully transfer the peppers to a bowl, or remove the basket from the pot and carefully pour the peppers into a bowl. Sprinkle with flaky sea salt and serve.

6–8 oz (170–225 g) shishito peppers

2 teaspoons olive oil

Kosher salt

Flaky sea salt

Awesome Onion Rings

If you're skeptical about how well onion rings can adapt to an air fryer, this recipe will win you over. Plain dried bread crumbs are the secret to producing the proper texture, and dipping the onions twice in an egg batter helps the breading stay on during cooking.

SERVES 2–4

In a medium bowl, whisk together the eggs and mayonnaise. Place the flour in a small bowl. In another medium bowl, stir together the bread crumbs, paprika, 1 teaspoon salt, and a few grindings of pepper.

Line a rimmed baking sheet with parchment paper. Working with 1 onion ring at a time, dip the ring in the egg mixture, letting the excess drip off, then dredge in the flour, shaking off the excess. Dip the ring in the egg mixture again, then dredge in the bread crumb mixture, pressing gently to adhere to both the outside and inside of the ring. Place the coated onion rings on the prepared baking sheet as you go.

Working in batches, coat the onion rings well with canola oil spray and arrange a single layer of rings in the Instant Pot® air fryer basket, making sure they don't touch. Insert the basket into the pot and attach the air fryer lid. Press the Air Fry button and set the cook time for 8 minutes at 350°F (180°C), then press Start. Flip the rings when prompted.

When the cooking time is up, if the rings aren't completely golden and crisp, cook for 2 minutes longer. Use tongs to carefully transfer the onion rings to a bowl. Repeat to cook the remaining batches, then serve.

3 large eggs

1 tablespoon mayonnaise

½ cup (2 oz/60 g) all-purpose flour

¾ cup (2¾ oz/75 g) plain dried bread crumbs

1 teaspoon smoked paprika

Kosher salt and freshly ground black pepper

½ cup all-purpose flour

1 large yellow or sweet onion, cut into ½-inch (12-mm) rings and separated

Fried Pickle Spears

This country-fair staple is now achievable at home with a simple beer batter and seasoned panko bread crumbs. Taste your pickles for saltiness since they vary from brand to brand. If they are on the saltier side, skip the salt in the bread crumb mixture.

SERVES 2–4

Cut the pickles lengthwise into thick spears and pat thoroughly dry with paper towels.

Spread the cornstarch on a plate. In a bowl, whisk together the flour, baking powder, and ½ teaspoon salt. Add the beer and water and whisk to combine; the batter should be thick but pourable. On another plate, stir together the bread crumbs, paprika, and 1 teaspoon salt, then transfer half the mixture to a small bowl and set aside.

Line a rimmed baking sheet with parchment paper. Working with a few spears at a time, coat the pickles in the cornstarch, shaking off the excess, then dip in the batter, letting the excess drip off. Dredge in the bread crumb mixture on the plate, turning to coat well and pressing gently to adhere. Place the coated pickles on the prepared baking sheet as you go. When the bread crumb mixture starts to become soggy, add the reserved mixture to the plate.

Working in batches, coat the pickles generously with canola oil spray and arrange a single layer of spears in the Instant Pot® air fryer basket, making sure they don't touch. Insert the basket into the pot and attach the air fryer lid. Press the Air Fry button and set the cook time for 8 minutes at 375°F (190°C), then press Start. Turn the spears when prompted, coating both sides again with oil.

When the cooking time is up, if the pickles are not deep golden brown and crisp, cook for 2 minutes longer. Use tongs to carefully transfer the pickles to a plate. Repeat to cook the remaining batches. Serve with spicy mayo alongside, if desired.

6 small dill pickles

¼ cup (1 oz/30 g) cornstarch

½ cup (2 oz/60 g) all-purpose flour

½ teaspoon baking powder

Kosher salt

¼ cup (60 ml) plus 2 tablespoons dark beer

5 tablespoons (75 ml) water

1½ cups (5¼ oz/150 g) panko bread crumbs

1 teaspoon paprika

Spicy Mayo (page 69), for serving (optional)

Mexican Corn on the Cob

Often referred to as Mexican street corn, this dish is irresistible when corn reaches its peak in summer. You'll need a few plates or trays to keep the multistep process organized, but the corn assembly line will be well worth it in the end. Serve with Crispy Fried Chicken Sandwiches (page 69) for the perfect outdoor picnic.

SERVES 4

Place the corn on a large plate or rimmed baking sheet and brush the ears with the melted butter. In a small bowl, stir together the chipotle chile powder, ¼ teaspoon salt, and a generous pinch of pepper. Sprinkle the spice mixture over the corn, rolling the ears to coat evenly.

Coat the Instant Pot® air fryer basket with canola oil spray and add 2 ears of corn. Insert the basket into the pot and attach the air fryer lid. Press the Air Fry button and set the cook time for 12 minutes at 400°F (200°C), then press Start. Rotate the corn when prompted.

Meanwhile, in a small bowl, stir together the mayonnaise, sour cream, and ½ teaspoon salt. Place half of the cheese on a large plate. Set aside.

When the cooking time is up, use tongs to carefully transfer the corn to a clean plate or rimmed baking sheet. Brush the corn with some of the sour cream mixture and let rest for 1 minute, allowing the mixture to be absorbed. Brush the corn again with more sour cream mixture, reserving about half for the remaining corn, then roll in the cheese to coat evenly. Sprinkle with chile powder and half of the cilantro.

Repeat to cook the remaining corn. Transfer the remaining cheese to the plate and coat the corn with the remaining sour cream mixture, cheese, chile powder, and cilantro. Serve with lime wedges alongside.

4 ears of yellow corn, shucked

2 tablespoons unsalted butter, melted

½ teaspoon chipotle chile powder, plus more for serving

Kosher salt and freshly ground black pepper

¼ cup (60 ml) mayonnaise

¼ cup (2 oz/60 g) sour cream

½ cup (2½ oz/70 g) Cotija cheese or queso fresco, crumbled

¼ cup (½ oz/15 g) chopped fresh cilantro

1 lime, cut into wedges

Crispy Brussels Sprouts with Honey-Lime Glaze

Oven-roasted brussels sprouts are often avoided (except on Thanksgiving, of course), because they seem to require more work than they should—and end up a soft, steamy mess without a lot of flavor. Thankfully, the solution is effortless: Plump, firm, and crunchy, these air-fried sprouts boast an incredible texture with a delectable spicy-sweet finish.

SERVES 2–4

In a large bowl, toss together the brussels sprouts, oil, red pepper flakes, and ¼ teaspoon salt.

Coat the Instant Pot® air fryer basket with canola oil spray and add the brussels sprouts. Insert the basket into the pot and attach the air fryer lid. Press the Air Fry button and set the cook time for 20 minutes at 350°F (180°C), then press Start. Toss the brussels sprouts when prompted.

Meanwhile, in a small bowl, stir together the honey, lime juice, and a generous pinch of salt. Set aside.

When the cooking time is up, use tongs to carefully transfer the brussels sprouts to a bowl, or remove the basket from the pot and carefully pour the brussels sprouts into a bowl. Drizzle with the honey-lime glaze, toss gently to coat (it's okay if some crispy outer leaves fall off in the process), and serve.

1 lb (450 g) brussels sprouts, trimmed and halved lengthwise (quartered if very large)

1 tablespoon olive oil

¼ teaspoon red pepper flakes

Kosher salt

2 tablespoons honey

Juice of 1 lime

Spicy Broccoli

Once you try this recipe, you'll find yourself saying all the time, "I could just air fry some broccoli to go with that." Twelve minutes and a spritz of olive oil are all you need to produce crunchy florets any night of the week. A pinch of red pepper flakes adds a hit of heat, but the broccoli is equally addictive without it.

SERVES 4

Place the broccoli in a large bowl and coat generously with olive oil spray. Sprinkle with ½ teaspoon salt and a pinch of red pepper flakes (or more, if you like more heat) and toss to coat.

Add the broccoli to the Instant Pot® air fryer basket. Insert the basket into the pot and attach the air fryer lid. Press the Air Fry button and set the cook time for 12 minutes at 400°F (200°C), then press Start. Toss the broccoli when prompted.

When the cooking time is up, if the broccoli is not crispy enough, add more cooking time in 2-minute intervals until the broccoli is cooked to the desired doneness. Use tongs to carefully transfer the broccoli to a bowl, or remove the basket from the pot and carefully pour the broccoli into a bowl, then serve.

1 lb (450 g) broccoli, cut into large florets

Kosher salt

Red pepper flakes

Perfect French Fries

Perhaps the holy grail of fried food, French fries really do live up to the hype of being able to be cooked in an air fryer with very little oil and a lot less fuss. The keys to success are cutting russet potatoes into ½-inch (12-mm) sticks, so they will be crispy on the outside and tender inside, and tossing them often during cooking to ensure even browning.

SERVES 4

Line a rimmed baking sheet with paper towels. Place the potatoes in a large colander and rinse under cold water until the water runs clear. Transfer the potatoes to a large bowl, cover with hot tap water, and let soak for 10 minutes. Drain the potatoes, then transfer to the prepared baking sheet. Place another layer of paper towels on top and pat the potatoes thoroughly dry.

Wipe the large bowl dry. Return the potatoes to the bowl, add the oil and ¼ teaspoon salt, and toss to coat evenly.

Coat the Instant Pot® air fryer basket with canola oil spray and add the potatoes. Insert the basket into the pot and attach the air fryer lid. Press the Air Fry button and set the cook time for 30 minutes at 375°F (190°C), then press Start. Toss the potatoes every 5–7 minutes so they brown evenly.

When the cooking time is up, use tongs to carefully transfer the potatoes to a bowl, or remove the basket from the pot and carefully pour the potatoes into a bowl. Sprinkle with salt and serve hot.

1 large or 2 medium russet potatoes cut into sticks ½ inch (12 mm) thick

1 tablespoon canola oil

Kosher salt

VARIATION

Parmesan Fries: *Prepare the fries as directed above and add them to the air fryer basket, setting the cook time for 25 minutes. When the cooking time is up, sprinkle the potatoes with 2 tablespoons freshly grated Parmesan cheese and cook for 5 minutes longer. Carefully transfer the potatoes to a bowl and sprinkle with 2 tablespoons grated Parmesan and 1 tablespoon chopped fresh flat-leaf parsley. Season with salt and a few grindings of pepper.*

Spicy Sweet Potato Wedges

Sweet potatoes are a fabulous superfood, but getting them to cook up crispy can be challenging. This is where air frying really shines, creating beautifully crisp skins and tender, sweet centers. We toss the potatoes with a simple blend of garlic powder, smoked paprika, salt, and pepper to pack a serious flavor punch.

SERVES 2–4

Using a sharp knife, cut the sweet potatoes into wedges about ½ inch (12 mm) thick and 3 inches (7.5 cm) long.

In a small bowl, stir together the garlic powder, paprika, ½ teaspoon salt, and ¼ teaspoon pepper. In a large bowl, toss together the sweet potatoes and oil. Sprinkle with the spice mixture and toss to coat.

Coat the Instant Pot® air fryer basket with canola oil spray and add half of the sweet potatoes. Insert the basket into the pot and attach the air fryer lid. Press the Air Fry button and set the cook time for 15 minutes at 400°F (200°C), then press Start. Toss the potatoes when prompted.

When the cooking time is up, use tongs to carefully transfer the potatoes to a bowl, or remove the basket from the pot and carefully pour the potatoes into a bowl. Repeat to cook the remaining batches, then serve.

1 large or 2 medium sweet potatoes (about 1 lb/450 g total), trimmed

1 teaspoon garlic powder

1 teaspoon smoked paprika

Kosher salt and freshly ground black pepper

1½ tablespoons olive oil

Classic Roast Potatoes

This versatile recipe works great for any variety of waxy potato and will accommodate a myriad of herb choices either during or after cooking. Keep batches small (no more than 1½ lb/680 g), and cut the potatoes into equal-size cubes (1–1½ inches/2.5–4 cm), and in just 20 minutes you'll savor absolutely amazing potatoes.

SERVES 4

In a large bowl, toss together the potatoes, oil, ½ teaspoon salt, and ⅛ teaspoon pepper.

Coat the Instant Pot® air fryer basket with canola oil spray and add the potatoes. Insert the basket into the pot and attach the air fryer lid. Press the Air Fry button and set the cook time for 20 minutes at 400°F (200°C), then press Start. Toss the potatoes when prompted.

When the cooking time is up, use tongs to carefully transfer the potatoes to a bowl, or remove the basket from the pot and carefully pour the potatoes into a bowl, then serve.

1½ lb (680 g) Yukon gold potatoes, cut into 1-inch (2.5-cm) cubes

1 tablespoon olive oil

Kosher salt and freshly ground black pepper

VARIATION

Herb-Roasted Potatoes: *Toss 2 tablespoons chopped fresh hearty herbs, such as oregano, thyme, or rosemary, with the potatoes, oil, salt, and pepper and cook as directed. To use fresh delicate herbs, such as parsley, dill, or tarragon, toss 1–2 tablespoons of them with the potatoes in the bowl after cooking.*

Smashed Potatoes

The Instant Pot® does double duty here by first pressure cooking the potatoes in just a few minutes (no heavy pots of boiling water to deal with), then crisping all the nooks and crannies of the smashed spuds. A sprinkle of good salt is all you'll need to finish them, or splurge with a drizzle of melted butter or a dunk in spicy mayo (page 69).

SERVES 4

Place the potatoes in the Instant Pot® air fryer basket. Pour 1½ cups (350 ml) water into the pot and insert the basket. Lock the pressure-cooking lid in place and turn the valve to sealing. Press the Pressure Cook button and set the cook time for 8 minutes at high pressure, then press Start.

When the cooking time is up, press the Quick Release Button or turn the valve to Venting to quick-release the steam. Carefully remove the lid. Remove the basket and drain the water from the pot. Press the Cancel button to reset the program

Pour the potatoes onto a rimmed baking sheet or cutting board and spread in a single layer. Using a meat pounder, potato masher, or hammer, carefully smash the potatoes to about ½ inch (12 mm) thick. Drizzle with the oil and sprinkle with ½ teaspoon salt and a few grindings of pepper. Using tongs, toss to coat.

Return the potatoes to the air fryer basket. Insert the basket into the pot and attach the air fryer lid. Press the Air Fry button and set the cook time for 20 minutes at 400°F (200°C), then press Start. Cook undisturbed.

When the cooking time is up, use tongs to carefully transfer the potatoes to a bowl, or remove the basket from the pot and carefully pour the potatoes into a bowl. Sprinkle with salt and serve.

1½ lb (680 g) small red potatoes, 1–1½ inches (2.5–4 cm) in diameter (cut larger potatoes in half)

1½ cups (350 ml) water

2 tablespoons olive oil

Kosher salt and freshly ground black pepper

Spiced Green Beans

A wonderful pantry staple, Old Bay seasoning doesn't get enough credit for its versatility and power-packed punch of flavor, spicing up more than just seafood. A sprinkle here transforms ordinary green beans into everyone's new favorite side dish—and a dash of Old Bay tossed with hot French fries (page 43) would be awesome, too.

SERVES 2–4

In a large bowl, toss together the green beans, oil, and Old Bay seasoning.

Coat the Instant Pot® air fryer basket with canola oil spray and add the beans. Insert the basket into the pot and attach the air fryer lid. Press the Broil button and set the cook time for 12 minutes at 400°F (200°C), then press Start. Toss the beans when prompted.

When the cooking time is up, use tongs to carefully transfer the beans to a bowl, or remove the basket from the pot and carefully pour the beans into a bowl.

1 lb (450 g) green beans, trimmed

1 teaspoon olive oil

½ teaspoon Old Bay seasoning

Zucchini Fries

Salting the zucchini spears before cooking helps remove excess moisture so they don't become mushy from the high heat. Use regular dried bread crumbs (not panko) for an extra-crispy coating that will stay put during cooking.

SERVES 4

In a large bowl, sprinkle the zucchini with the lemon zest and ½ teaspoon salt. Let stand at room temperature for 10 minutes.

Using paper towels, gently blot the zucchini to remove excess moisture, being careful to not wipe off the lemon zest. In a medium bowl, whisk together the eggs and water. In another large bowl or on a plate, stir together the bread crumbs and cheese.

Line a rimmed baking sheet with parchment paper. Working with a few pieces at a time, dip the zucchini in the egg mixture, letting the excess drip off, then dredge in the bread crumb mixture, turning to coat well and pressing gently to adhere. Place the coated zucchini on the prepared baking sheet as you go.

Coat the Instant Pot® air fryer basket with canola oil spray. Working in batches, coat the zucchini generously with canola oil spray and arrange a single layer of pieces in the basket, making sure they don't touch. Insert the basket into the pot and attach the air fryer lid. Press the Air Fry button and set the cook time for 8 minutes at 400°F (200°C), then press Start. Toss the zucchini when prompted, coating both sides again with oil.

Meanwhile, make the garlic aioli: In a medium bowl, whisk together the egg yolk and water until frothy. While whisking constantly, add the canola oil in a slow, steady stream, followed by the olive oil, until the mixture thickens. Stir in the lemon juice and garlic and season to taste with salt. Refrigerate until ready to use.

When the cooking time is up, use tongs to transfer the zucchini to a bowl. Repeat to cook the remaining batches. Serve with the garlic aioli or marinara sauce (page 135) alongside for dipping.

2 zucchini, cut into spears 3 inches (7.5 cm) long and 1 inch (2.5 cm) thick

½ teaspoon freshly grated lemon zest

Kosher salt

2 large eggs

1 tablespoon water

1 cup (3½ oz/100 g) plain dried bread crumbs

3 tablespoons freshly grated Parmesan cheese

FOR THE GARLIC AIOLI

1 large egg yolk

1 teaspoon water

⅓ cup (80 ml) canola oil

¼ cup (60 ml) olive oil

2 teaspoons fresh lemon juice

1 clove garlic, minced

Kosher salt

Crispy Chickpeas

Re-creating this addictive snack in the air fryer is easy: Pressure cook dried beans, then fry them in a blend of paprika, cumin, and cayenne. Both steps take some time, but it's all hands-off cooking so you can relax and mix up some cocktails while you wait.

SERVES 4

Combine the chickpeas, water, canola oil, and 1 teaspoon salt in the Instant Pot®. Lock the pressure-cooking lid in place and turn the valve to Sealing. Press the Pressure Cook button and set the cook time for 35 minutes at high pressure, then press Start.

When the cooking time is up, let the steam release naturally for 10 minutes, then press the Quick Release Button or turn the valve to Venting to quick-release any residual steam. Carefully remove the lid and drain the chickpeas in a colander set in the sink. Press the Cancel button to reset the program.

In a large bowl, toss together the chickpeas, olive oil, paprika, cumin, cayenne, and ½ teaspoon salt. Add the chickpeas to the Instant Pot® air fryer basket. Insert the basket into the pot and attach the air fryer lid. Press the Air Fry button and set the cook time for 25 minutes at 390°F (199°C), then press Start. Gently toss the chickpeas when prompted.

When the cooking time is up, if the chickpeas aren't crispy enough, add more cooking time in 2-minute intervals until the chickpeas are cooked to the desired crispness. Carefully remove the basket from the pot and pour the chickpeas into a bowl. Taste and adjust the seasoning with salt and serve.

NOTE *To save time, you can use 1 can (15 oz) of cooked chickpeas instead. Drain and rinse the chickpeas, dry well with paper towels, then toss with the olive oil and seasonings. Add to the air fryer basket, setting the cook time for 18–20 minutes at 375°F (190°C).*

1 cup (7 oz/200 g) dried chickpeas, rinsed and picked over

4 cups (950 ml) water

1 teaspoon canola oil

Kosher salt

1 tablespoon olive oil

1 teaspoon paprika

½ teaspoon ground cumin

Pinch of cayenne pepper

BBQ Chicken Drumsticks (page 82)

MAIN DISHES

Apricot-Ginger Glazed Pork Chops

Brushing meat with a jam-based glaze is a genius way to contribute color and flavor to a dish. A second coating of glaze after cooking adds extra zing and a shiny finish. Round out the meal with Classic Roast Potatoes (page 46) or Smashed Potatoes (page 47).

SERVES 2

Pat the pork chops dry with paper towels. Season generously with salt and pepper. In a small bowl, stir together the jam and ginger; if desired, reserve some of the glaze for serving. Brush the chops on both sides with the glaze.

Coat the Instant Pot® air fryer basket with canola oil spray. Place the pork chops in the basket, making sure they don't touch. Insert the basket into the pot and attach the air fryer lid. Press the Air Fry button and set the cook time for 18 minutes at 350°F (180°C), then press Start. Flip the pork chops when prompted, brushing with more glaze when flipping.

When the cooking time is up, insert an instant-read thermometer into the thickest part of the pork, away from the bone; it should register 140°F (60°C). If the pork is not fully cooked, add more cooking time in 2-minute intervals until the pork is fully cooked. Use tongs to carefully transfer the pork to a plate. Brush with more glaze, if desired, and serve.

2 bone-in pork chops (each ½–¾ lb/225–340 g and about 1 inch/2.5 cm) thick

Kosher salt and freshly ground black pepper

3 tablespoons apricot jam

3 teaspoons peeled and grated fresh ginger

Peach jam would also be delicious as a glaze for these juicy chops.

Asian-Style Pork Ribs

When pork ribs are pressure cooked and then broiled, fall-off-the-bone meat is coated in a sweet and tangy sauce and then crisped to perfection, all in the same appliance. This homemade Asian-inspired barbecue sauce would also be delicious on chicken wings (page 30) or drumsticks (page 82).

SERVES 4–6

In a bowl, whisk together the marinade ingredients.

Place the ribs in a large lock-top plastic bag and pour in the marinade. Seal the bag, massaging the marinade around the ribs. Refrigerate overnight.

Remove the ribs from the marinade and place them in the Instant Pot®, standing the racks upright around the edge of the pot (it's okay if they overlap). Pour the marinade over the ribs and into the center of the pot. Lock the pressure-cooking lid in place and turn the valve to Sealing. Press the Pressure Cook button and set the cook time for 30 minutes at high pressure, then press Start.

To make the sauce, in a bowl, whisk together the hoisin sauce, chili sauce, mirin, and sesame oil. Taste and add more sesame oil, if desired.

When the cooking time is up, let the steam release naturally for 15 minutes, then press the Quick Release Button or turn the valve to Venting to quick-release any residual steam. Carefully remove the lid. Use tongs to transfer the ribs to a cutting board. Drain the liquid from the pot. Press the Cancel button to reset the program.

Cut the racks into individual ribs and brush generously with sauce. Coat the air fryer basket with canola oil spray. Arrange half of the ribs in a single layer in the basket, standing them upright on their sides. Insert the basket into the pot and attach the air fryer lid. Press the Broil button and set the cook time for 8 minutes at 400°F (200°C), then press Start. Cook undisturbed.

When the cooking time is up, use tongs to carefully transfer the ribs to a platter and brush with more sauce while hot. Repeat to cook the remaining ribs, then brush with sauce and serve.

FOR THE MARINADE

½ cup (120 ml) soy sauce

¼ cup (2 oz/60 g) firmly packed light brown sugar

2 tablespoons rice vinegar

2 tablespoons toasted sesame oil

2 tablespoons minced garlic

1 tablespoon peeled and grated fresh ginger

1 tablespoon ketchup

1½ teaspoons Chinese five-spice powder

1 teaspoon red pepper flakes

4–5 lb (1.8–2.3 kg) St. Louis–style pork ribs, cut into racks of about 6 ribs each

FOR THE SAUCE

½ cup (120 ml) hoisin sauce

⅓ cup (80 ml) Thai sweet chili sauce

2 tablespoons mirin

1 tablespoon toasted sesame oil, plus more as needed

Cajun-Rubbed Pork Tenderloin

Rubbing a tender cut of pork with a simple spice blend yields an impressive weeknight dinner when served with creamy polenta (page 135) and a side salad. Since a tenderloin is often quite long, cut it in half crosswise and place the pieces side by side in the air fryer basket. Then transform leftovers into a Cubano sandwich the next day (see note below).

SERVES 4

Pat the pork tenderloin dry with paper towels. Rub each piece with 1 teaspoon of the oil.

In a small bowl, whisk together the Cajun seasoning, brown sugar, ½ teaspoon salt, and ¼ teaspoon pepper. Sprinkle the pork evenly on all sides with the rub.

Coat the Instant Pot® air fryer basket with canola oil spray. Place the pork pieces in the basket, making sure they don't touch. Insert the basket into the pot and attach the air fryer lid. Press the Air Fry button and set the cook time for 20 minutes at 350°F (180°C), then press Start. Rotate the pork pieces when prompted.

When the cooking time is up, insert an instant-read thermometer into the thickest part of the pork; it should register 140°F (60°C). If the pork is not fully cooked, add more cooking time in 2-minute intervals until the pork is fully cooked. Use tongs to carefully transfer the pork to a cutting board and let rest for 5–10 minutes, then cut into slices. Serve over a bowl of polenta, if desired.

IF YOU HAVE LEFTOVERS

Sliced pork tenderloin makes an excellent filling for Cuban sandwiches. Layer the pork with slices of Swiss cheese, pickles, ham, and mustard on long sandwich rolls. Cut the sandwich in half, spread the tops of each half with softened butter, and place in the air fryer basket. (Use a piece of aluminum foil underneath to prevent a cheesy mess.) Press the Air Fry button and set the cook time for 5 minutes at 375°F (190°C) (or until the cheese is melted), then press Start.

1 lb (450 g) pork tenderloin, cut crosswise into 2 pieces

2 teaspoons canola oil

1 tablespoon Cajun seasoning

1 tablespoon firmly packed light brown sugar

Kosher salt and freshly ground black pepper

Polenta (page 135), for serving (optional)

Pork Schnitzel

Super-thin, breaded pork chops cook in under 10 minutes in the air fryer, making this a fast weeknight dinner for one or many. If preparing 4 chops, increase the breading quantities to ½ cup (2 oz/60 g) flour, 3 eggs mixed with 3 tablespoons water, and 2 cups (7 oz/200 g) panko. Because the pounded chops are quite large, you can cook only one at a time.

SERVES 2

Place a piece of plastic wrap on a cutting board and set the pork chops on top. Cover the pork with another piece of plastic wrap. Using a meat pounder, rolling pin, or hammer, gently pound the pork flat, working from the center outward and stretching the pork chops as you pound, so they are just slightly thicker than ¼ inch (6 mm). Transfer to a plate.

In a medium bowl, whisk together the flour, 1 teaspoon salt, ¼ teaspoon black pepper, and cayenne (if using). In a large, shallow bowl, whisk together the eggs and water. Place the bread crumbs in another medium bowl or on a large plate.

Line a rimmed baking sheet with parchment paper. Pat the pork chops dry with paper towels. Working with 1 chop at a time, coat the pork in the flour mixture, shaking off the excess. Dip in the egg mixture, letting the excess drip off, then dredge in the bread crumbs, turning to coat well and pressing gently to adhere. Place the coated chops on the prepared baking sheet as you go.

Coat the Instant Pot® air fryer basket with canola oil spray. Coat 1 chop generously with olive oil spray and place in the basket. Insert the basket into the pot and attach the air fryer lid. Press the Air Fry button and set the cook time for 9 minutes at 400°F (200°C), then press Start. Flip the chop when prompted.

When the cooking time is up, insert an instant-read thermometer into the thickest part of the chop; it should register 140°F (60°C) and the chop should be golden and crispy. If it is not, add more cooking time in 2-minute intervals until the pork is fully cooked. Use tongs to carefully transfer the pork to a plate. Repeat to cook the remaining chop, then serve.

2 boneless pork chops (each about ¼ lb/115 g)

⅓ cup (1½ oz/40 g) all-purpose flour

Kosher salt and freshly ground black pepper

¼ teaspoon cayenne pepper (optional)

2 large eggs

1 tablespoon water

1 cup (3½ oz/100 g) panko bread crumbs

Soy-Honey Glazed Pork Meatballs

These sweet and salty meatballs are wonderful for dinner served over a bowl of rice (page 136) with your favorite veggies or as an appetizer at a party.

SERVES 2–4

In a bowl, combine the pork, green onions, ginger, garlic, soy sauce, ½ teaspoon salt, and a few grindings of pepper. Mix gently with your hands or a wooden spoon until just combined (be careful not to overmix or the meat will become tough), making sure the onions are evenly distributed.

Line a rimmed baking sheet with parchment paper. Pour the oil into a small bowl. Use a small ice cream scoop about 1½ inches (4 cm) in diameter or a tablespoon measure to scoop the meat mixture into equal-size balls. Place on the prepared baking sheet. Coat your palms and fingertips lightly with the oil. Roll each ball between your palms until smooth and evenly rounded. (The meatballs should be well oiled and shiny.)

Coat the Instant Pot® air fryer basket with canola oil spray. Working in batches, arrange a single layer of meatballs in the basket, making sure they don't touch. Insert the basket into the pot and attach the air fryer lid. Press the Air Fry button and set the cook time for 10 minutes at 375°F (190°C), then press Start. Rotate the meatballs when prompted.

1 lb (450 g) ground pork

2 green onions, white and pale green parts, finely chopped

2 teaspoons peeled and minced or grated fresh ginger

2 cloves garlic, minced or grated

1 tablespoon soy sauce

Kosher salt and freshly ground black pepper

1 tablespoon olive oil

The irresistible soy-honey glaze becomes sticky when cooled, making a mouthwatering combo paired with the delicate meatballs.

Meanwhile, make the soy-honey glaze: In a small saucepan over medium-high heat, stir together the honey, soy sauce, mirin, garlic, ginger, and ¼ teaspoon salt. Bring to a boil, stirring occasionally, then remove from the heat and let stand for 5 minutes. Place a fine-mesh sieve over a glass measuring cup and strain the glaze. Set aside.

When the cooking time is up, use tongs to carefully transfer the meatballs to a plate. Alternatively, place on a baking sheet in a 250°F (120°C) oven to keep warm. Repeat to cook the remaining batches.

Divide the rice among bowls and top with the meatballs. Drizzle with the glaze, sprinkle with sesame seeds, and serve.

TIP *Coating a measuring cup with canola oil spray before measuring the honey for the glaze will help it slide into the saucepan.*

FOR THE SOY-HONEY GLAZE
⅓ **cup (4 oz/115 g) honey**

1 tablespoon soy sauce

1 tablespoon sake or mirin

4 cloves garlic, smashed

1-inch (2.5-cm) piece fresh ginger, unpeeled, sliced and smashed

Kosher salt

FOR SERVING
Cooked rice (page 136)

Toasted sesame seeds

Sunday Roast with Classic Roast Potatoes

If you've had a "Sunday lunch" in England, you may remember beautifully cooked roast beef paired with crispy roast potatoes and horseradish cream sauce. Now you can create that traditional meal at home in the Instant Pot®. Drizzling the cooked roast with butter and honey might seem a little indulgent, but the creamy-sweet combo is a brilliant finish for the well-seasoned meat.

SERVES 4-6

In a mortar with a pestle, or in a small bowl using the handle of a wooden spoon, grind together the rosemary, 1½ teaspoons salt, and the peppercorns. The mixture should be chunky. Pat the roast dry with paper towels. Rub the meat all over with ½–1 tablespoon oil (depending on the size of the roast) and sprinkle the seasoning on all sides.

Coat the Instant Pot® air fryer basket with canola oil spray. Place the roast in the center of the basket. Insert the basket into the pot and attach the air fryer lid. Press the Air Fry button and set the cook time for 16–18 minutes per pound of meat at 325°F (165°C) (start with the lower amount of time and add more time if needed), then press Start. Turn the meat when prompted.

Meanwhile, make the horseradish cream: In a small bowl, stir together the sour cream, horseradish, and ¼ teaspoon salt. Taste and adjust the seasoning with salt. Cover and refrigerate until ready to use.

When the cooking time is up, insert an instant-read thermometer into the center of the meat; it should register 130°–135°F (54°–57°C) for medium-rare and 135°–145°F (57°–63°C) for medium. If the roast is not cooked to the desired doneness, add more cooking time in 2-minute intervals. Use tongs to transfer the roast to a cutting board. Place 1–2 tablespoons butter on top (depending on the size of the roast) and let it melt. Drizzle with the honey, cover loosely with aluminum foil, and let rest for 15–20 minutes.

While the meat rests, cook the potatoes. Cut the roast into thin, round slices and serve with the horseradish cream and potatoes alongside.

1 tablespoon loosely packed fresh rosemary leaves

Kosher salt

1 teaspoon black or pink peppercorns

1 eye of round roast (2–3 lb/1–1.4 kg)

½–1 tablespoon olive oil

1–2 tablespoons unsalted butter

FOR THE HORSERADISH CREAM
⅓ cup (2½ oz/70 g) sour cream

1½ tablespoons prepared horseradish

Kosher salt

1 tablespoon honey

Classic Roast Potatoes (page 46)

Be sure the meat fits in your air fryer basket before cooking.

Cheese-Stuffed Beef Burgers

The Midwest is famous for its messy burgers with cheesy centers. For this version, sharp Cheddar balances the richness of the meat. Be sure to make an indentation with your thumb in the center of the patty to keep it from puffing as it cooks. Toppings take this sandwich to the next level—start with lettuce, tomatoes, pickles, spicy mayo, and ketchup and mustard, of course, then get creative.

SERVES 2

In a bowl, combine the beef, garlic powder, onion powder, ½ teaspoon salt, and a few grindings of pepper and mix gently with your hands or a wooden spoon until just combined (be careful not to overmix or the meat will become tough). Divide the meat mixture into 2 patties, each about 5 inches (13 cm) in diameter and 1 inch (2.5 cm) thick.

Place half of the cheese in the center of each patty and shape the meat into a ball to enclose the cheese, then reshape into 5-by-1-inch (13-by-2.5-cm) patties. Use your thumb to make an indentation in the center of each patty (this will prevent them from puffing up during cooking).

Coat the Instant Pot® air fryer basket with canola oil spray. Arrange the patties in a single layer in the basket, making sure they don't touch. Insert the basket into the pot and attach the air fryer lid. Press the Air Fry button and set the cook time for 8 minutes (for medium) or 9 minutes (for medium-well) at 400°F (200°C), then press Start. Flip the burgers when prompted.

When the cooking time is up, use a nonstick spatula to carefully transfer the burgers to a plate.

Place 1 bun, cut-sides down, on the dehydrating tray, insert the tray into the basket, and attach the air fryer lid. Press the Air Fry button and set the cook time for 2 minutes at 400°F (200°C), then press Start. Use tongs to transfer the bun to a plate. Repeat to toast the remaining bun.

Place the burgers on the buns, add the desired toppings, and serve.

¾ lb (340 g) 85% lean ground beef

½ teaspoon garlic powder

½ teaspoon onion powder

Kosher salt and freshly ground black pepper

2 oz (60 g) Cheddar cheese, preferably sharp, shredded

2 brioche buns (page 118 or store-bought)

FOR SERVING
Lettuce, tomato slices, pickle slices, mayonnaise or Spicy Mayo (page 69), mustard, ketchup

Korean BBQ Flank Steak

A Korean fermented chile paste, gochujang is combined here with garlic, ginger, soy sauce, rice vinegar, and brown sugar, taking this simple marinade for flank steak to the next level. The meat turns lusciously salty-sweet with a crispy crust when broiled. Serve the succulent slices with rice and your favorite vegetable. Leftovers are wonderful with eggs for breakfast or atop a rice bowl for lunch.

SERVES 2–4

In a glass measuring cup or small bowl, whisk together the soy sauce, vinegar, brown sugar, gochujang, garlic, and ginger. Place the steak in a large lock-top plastic bag or a shallow baking dish just large enough to hold it and pour the marinade over the meat. Seal the bag or cover the dish with plastic wrap and let stand at room temperature for 30 minutes or refrigerate up to overnight, turning occasionally. If refrigerated, let stand at room temperature for about 30 minutes before cooking.

Coat the Instant Pot® air fryer basket with canola oil spray. Working in batches if needed, remove the steak from the marinade, letting the excess drip off, and place in the basket. If the steak is too big to fit in the basket in 1 piece, cut it in half crosswise, making sure the pieces don't touch. Insert the basket into the pot and attach the air fryer lid. Press the Broil button and set the cook time for 10 minutes at 400°F (200°C), then press Start. Flip the steak halfway through the cooking time.

When the cooking time is up, insert an instant-read thermometer into the thickest part of the meat; it should register 130°–135°F (54°–57°C) for medium-rare and 135°–145°F (57°–63°C) for medium. If the steak is not cooked to the desired doneness, add more cooking time in 2-minute intervals until the steak is cooked as desired. Use tongs to carefully transfer the steak to a cutting board and let rest for 5–10 minutes, then cut across the grain into slices. If cooking in batches, repeat to cook the remaining piece, then serve.

NOTE *Flank steak is sold in a range of sizes and weights. The marinade in this recipe will cover up to 1½ lb (680 g) of meat, so if your piece is large, cut it in half to fit in the basket and cook the meat in 2 batches.*

3 tablespoons soy sauce

1 tablespoon rice vinegar

¼ cup (2 oz/60 g) firmly packed light brown sugar

1 tablespoon gochujang (Korean chile paste)

2 cloves garlic, grated

1 teaspoon peeled and grated fresh ginger

1 flank steak (¾–1½ lb/ 340–680 g and about 1 inch/2.5 cm thick)

Balsamic-Honey Marinated Sirloin Steak

This easy marinade caramelizes beautifully on the beef as it cooks, becoming just crispy enough without burning. If your steak is too large to fit into the pot, cut it in half crosswise and cook in batches. As an added bonus, the second steak will soak up some of the residual marinade from the first and caramelize even more.

SERVES 4

In a small bowl, whisk together the vinegar, honey, oil, and 1 tablespoon pepper. Place the steak in a large lock-top plastic bag or shallow baking dish just large enough to hold it and pour the marinade over the meat. Let stand at room temperature for 1–2 hours, turning occasionally.

Coat the Instant Pot® air fryer basket with canola oil spray. Remove the steak from the marinade, letting the excess drip off, and season generously on both sides with salt. If the steak is too big to fit in the basket in 1 piece, cut it in half crosswise. Arrange the pieces in a single layer in the basket, angling them in so they don't touch. (If the pieces are too big to fit together without touching, cook in 2 batches.) Insert the basket into the pot and attach the air fryer lid. Press the Broil button and set the cook time for 10 minutes at 400°F (200°C), then press Start. Flip the steak when prompted.

When the cooking time is up, insert an instant-read thermometer into the thickest part of the meat; it should register 130°–135°F (54°–57°C) for medium-rare and 135°–145°F (57°–63°C) for medium. If the steak is not cooked to the desired doneness, add more cooking time in 2-minute intervals until the steak is cooked as desired. Use tongs to carefully transfer the steak to a cutting board and let rest for 5–10 minutes, then cut across the grain into slices. If cooking in batches, repeat to cook the remaining piece, then serve.

¼ cup (60 ml) balsamic vinegar

2 tablespoons honey

2 tablespoons olive oil

Kosher salt and freshly ground black pepper

1 sirloin steak (1–1½ lb/ 450–680 g and 1–1½ inches/ 2.5–4 cm thick)

Chicken Taquitos

Fill these Mexican-inspired rollups with any of your favorite taco toppings—cheese and cilantro are just the beginning. Pico de Gallo is great for dipping, but any fresh salsa or guacamole would be a wonderful match as well. Use corn or flour tortillas—melted butter is the secret to holding them together and creating a crisp, golden crust.

SERVES 4–6

In a small bowl, whisk together the cumin, chili powder, 1 teaspoon salt, and a few grindings of pepper.

Pat the chicken dry with paper towels and place in a bowl. Rub with the oil, then sprinkle with the spice mixture and toss to coat.

Coat the Instant Pot® air fryer basket with canola oil spray. Working in batches, arrange a single layer of thighs in the basket, making sure they don't touch. Insert the basket into the pot and attach the air fryer lid. Press the Broil button and set the cook time for 14 minutes at 400°F (200°C), then press Start. Flip the chicken when prompted.

When the cooking time is up, use tongs to carefully transfer the chicken to a cutting board. Shred or cut into strips.

Place a tortilla on a work surface and sprinkle a few tablespoons of the cheese in the center, leaving at least a 1-inch (2.5-cm) border all around the cheese. Top with chicken, lime juice, and cilantro. Roll the tortilla tightly, tucking in the filling. Brush the seam with a little melted butter to seal, then place it, seam-side down, on a plate. Repeat to roll the remaining taquitos.

Working in batches, brush the taquitos generously on both sides with the remaining melted butter, then place them, seam-side down, on the dehydrating tray. (It's okay if they touch; you should be able to fit 3 or 4 on the tray at one time.) Insert the tray into the air fryer basket and attach the air fryer lid. Press the Air Fry button and set the cook time for 5 minutes at 400°F (200°C), then press Start. Cook undisturbed.

Use tongs to carefully transfer the taquitos to a plate. Repeat to cook the remaining batches. Serve with pico de gallo alongside for dipping.

1½ tablespoons ground cumin

2 teaspoons chili powder

Kosher salt and freshly ground black pepper

6 boneless, skinless chicken thighs (1½–2 lb/680 g–1 kg total)

2 teaspoons canola oil

12 (6-inch/15-cm) corn or flour tortillas

2 cups (8 oz/225 g) shredded Monterey jack or pepper jack cheese, or Mexican blend shredded cheese

1 lime, cut into wedges

¼ cup (½ oz/15 g) chopped fresh cilantro

2 tablespoons unsalted butter, melted

Pico de Gallo (page 91), for serving

Try the spicy mayo as a dipping sauce for Classic Roast Potatoes (page 46).

Crispy Fried Chicken Sandwiches

Crunchy, juicy, spicy, and satisfying, these crave-worthy sandwiches check all the boxes when it comes to healthier fried food. Rice flour provides a barrier between the extreme heat and tender chicken, helping to keep the meat moist inside and crispy outside. Add more hot sauce and/or cayenne pepper if you like it hot—the crunchy cabbage and cooling pickles balance the spicy richness of the sandwich.

SERVES 4-6

In a medium bowl, whisk together the rice flour, baking powder, 2 teaspoons salt, and 1 teaspoon black pepper. In another medium bowl, whisk together the buttermilk, eggs, cayenne, and hot pepper sauce (if using).

Line a rimmed baking sheet with parchment paper. Pat the chicken dry with paper towels. Working with a few thighs at a time, coat the chicken in the rice flour mixture, shaking off the excess. Dip in the buttermilk mixture, letting the excess drip off. Transfer again to the flour mixture, turning to coat well and pressing gently to cover all the nooks and crannies. Place the coated chicken on the prepared baking sheet as you go.

Coat the Instant Pot® air fryer basket with canola oil spray. Working in batches, coat the chicken generously with olive oil spray and arrange a single layer of thighs in the basket, making sure they don't touch. Insert the basket into the pot and attach the air fryer lid. Press the Air Fry button and set the cook time for 14 minutes at 400°F (200°C), then press Start. Flip the chicken when prompted, coating both sides again with olive oil.

Meanwhile, make the spicy mayo: In a small bowl, stir together the mayonnaise, Sriracha, and cayenne. Set aside.

When the cooking time is up, use tongs to carefully transfer the chicken to a plate. Repeat to cook the remaining batches.

Spread a thin layer of the spicy mayo on the inside of the brioche buns. Top the bottom half of each bun with a piece of chicken, pickles, and shredded cabbage. Cover with the top of the buns and serve.

2 cups (10 oz/285 g) rice flour

1 tablespoon baking powder

Kosher salt and freshly ground black pepper

1 cup (240 ml) buttermilk, preferably full-fat

2 large eggs

½ teaspoon cayenne pepper

1 teaspoon hot pepper sauce (optional)

1–1½ lb (450–680 g) boneless, skinless chicken thighs (4–6)

FOR THE SPICY MAYO
¾ cup (180 ml) mayonnaise

1 tablespoon Sriracha or other hot sauce

Pinch of cayenne pepper

FOR SERVING
4–6 brioche buns (page 118 or store-bought)

Sliced bread and butter pickles, shredded red or green cabbage

Buttermilk Fried Chicken

This was by far the most intimidating dish to attempt in an air fryer, mostly because it's such a quintessential deep-fried food. But this method incorporates many of the same classic fried chicken techniques, including an overnight soak in buttermilk, lots of fragrant spices, and a good dredge in a flour-cornstarch mixture. Coat the pieces well with canola oil spray, but there's no need to flip them during cooking.

SERVES 4–6

To make the spice mixture, in a small bowl, whisk together 2 tablespoons black pepper, the paprika, brown sugar, garlic, oregano, and cayenne.

In a large bowl, whisk together the buttermilk, egg, 1 tablespoon salt, and 2 tablespoons of the spice mixture (reserve the remaining spice mixture). Place the chicken in a large lock-top plastic bag, then pour the marinade into the bag. Seal the bag, massaging the marinade around the chicken. Refrigerate for at least 4 hours or up to overnight.

In a large bowl, whisk together the flour, cornstarch, baking powder, 2 teaspoons salt, and the reserved spice mixture.

Line a rimmed baking sheet with parchment paper. Working with 1 thigh at a time, remove the chicken from the marinade, letting the excess drip off, then coat in the flour mixture, shaking off the excess. Place the coated chicken on the prepared baking sheet as you go.

Coat the Instant Pot® air fryer basket with canola oil spray. Working in batches, coat the chicken generously with canola oil spray and arrange a single layer of thighs in the basket, making sure they don't touch. Insert the basket into the pot and attach the air fryer lid. Press the Air Fry button and set the cook time for 25 minutes at 400°F (200°C), then press Start. Cook undisturbed.

When the cooking time is up, insert an instant-read thermometer into the center of a thigh, away from the bone; it should register 175°F (80°C). If the chicken is not fully cooked, add more cooking time in 2-minute intervals. Repeat to cook the remaining batches, then serve.

FOR THE SPICE MIXTURE
Freshly ground black pepper

1 tablespoon smoked paprika

1 tablespoon firmly packed light brown sugar

2 teaspoons granulated garlic

2 teaspoons dried oregano

½ teaspoon cayenne pepper

1 cup (240 ml) buttermilk, preferably full-fat

1 large egg

Kosher salt

3 lb (1.4 kg) bone-in, skin-on chicken thighs

1 cup (4 oz/115 g) all-purpose flour

¼ cup (1 oz/30 g) cornstarch

1 teaspoon baking powder

Classic Chicken Nuggets

Even the pickiest little eaters will devour these crunchy, flavor-packed chicken bites. The recipe yields a good-size batch, so refrigerate leftover cooked nuggets for up to 5 days; reheat in the air fryer at 350°F (180°C) for 5 minutes. You can also freeze uncooked breaded chicken in a single layer on a rimmed baking sheet for about 2 hours, then transfer to a lock-top plastic bag and freeze for up to 3 months.

SERVES 4

Place the flour in a medium bowl. In a large, shallow bowl, whisk together the eggs and water. In another medium bowl or on a large plate, stir together the bread crumbs, cheese, oregano, 1½ teaspoons salt, and ½ teaspoon pepper.

Line a rimmed baking sheet with parchment paper. Pat the chicken dry with paper towels. Season lightly with salt and pepper. Working with a few pieces at a time, coat the chicken in flour, shaking off the excess. Dip in the egg mixture, letting the excess drip off, then dredge in the bread crumb mixture, turning to coat well and pressing gently to adhere. Place the coated chicken on the prepared baking sheet as you go.

Coat the Instant Pot® air fryer basket with canola oil spray. Working in batches, coat the chicken generously with canola oil spray and arrange a single layer of pieces in the basket, making sure they don't touch. Insert the basket into the pot and attach the air fryer lid. Press the Air Fry button and set the cook time for 10 minutes at 400°F (200°C), then press Start. Flip the chicken when prompted, coating both sides again with oil.

When the cooking time is up, use tongs to carefully transfer the chicken nuggets to a plate. Alternatively, place on a baking sheet in a 250°F (120°C) oven to keep warm. Repeat to cook the remaining batches. Serve with the sauce(s) alongside for dipping.

NOTE *Thick chicken breasts work best for this recipe. If you buy chicken breasts with the tenders still attached, cut them off, keeping them in one piece, and coat and cook them the same way.*

⅓ **cup (1½ oz/40 g) all-purpose flour**

2 large eggs

1 tablespoon water

1½ cups (5¼ oz/150 g) panko bread crumbs

¼ **cup (1 oz/30 g) freshly grated Parmesan cheese**

1 teaspoon dried oregano

Kosher salt and freshly ground black pepper

2 lb (1 kg) boneless, skinless chicken breasts (about 4), cut into 1½-inch (4-cm) chunks (see note)

BBQ Sauce (page 82) or Honey-Mustard Sauce (page 80), for serving

Chicken Parmesan

No frying pans, baking dishes, or layers of paper towels are needed for this beloved Italian-American classic. Super-thin chicken breasts crisp to perfection in the air fryer basket, then the cheese melts quickly on top using the dehydrating tray, which allows the food to be closer to the pot's heating element. The results are equally delicious served as a sandwich, either with or without a quick marinara sauce.

SERVES 4

Place a piece of plastic wrap on a cutting board and set 2 chicken breasts on top. Cover the chicken with another piece of plastic wrap. Using a meat pounder, rolling pin, or hammer, gently pound the chicken flat, working from the center outward and stretching the chicken breast as you pound, until it is just slightly thicker than ¼ inch (6 mm). Transfer to a plate. Repeat with the remaining 2 chicken breasts, using fresh sheets of plastic wrap if needed.

In a medium bowl, whisk together the flour, garlic powder, 1 teaspoon salt, and ½ teaspoon pepper. In another medium bowl, whisk together the eggs and water. In a large bowl or on a plate, stir together the bread crumbs, Parmesan, and parsley.

Line a rimmed baking sheet with parchment paper. Pat the chicken dry with paper towels. Coat the chicken in the flour mixture, shaking off the excess. Dip in the egg mixture, letting the excess drip off, then dredge in the bread crumb mixture, turning to coat well and pressing gently to cover all the nooks and crannies. Place the coated chicken on the prepared baking sheet as you go.

Coat the Instant Pot® air fryer basket with canola oil spray. Working in batches, coat the chicken generously with olive oil spray and arrange a single layer of breasts in the basket, making sure they don't touch. Insert the basket into the pot and attach the air fryer lid. Press the Air Fry button and set the cook time for 9 minutes at 400°F (200°C), then press Start. Flip the chicken when prompted, coating both sides again with olive oil.

4 boneless, skinless chicken breasts (1–1½ lb/450–680 g total and ½ inch/12 mm thick), or 2 large, thick breasts, halved lengthwise horizontally (see note)

¼ cup (1 oz/30 g) all-purpose flour

2 teaspoons garlic powder

Kosher salt and freshly ground black pepper

2 large eggs

1 tablespoon water

1 cup (3½ oz/100 g) panko bread crumbs

⅓ cup (1½ oz/40 g) freshly grated Parmesan or pecorino romano cheese

2 tablespoons chopped fresh flat-leaf parsley

This easy and flavorful marinara sauce takes only 5 minutes to cook in the Instant Pot®.

continued from page 72

When the cooking time is up, use tongs to carefully transfer the chicken to a plate. Alternatively, place on a baking sheet in a 250°F (120°C) oven to keep warm. Repeat to cook the remaining batches.

Place 2 chicken breasts on the dehydrating tray and insert the tray into the air fryer basket. Top each breast with a piece of cheese. Attach the air fryer lid. Press the Broil button and set the cook time for 3 minutes at 400°F (200°C), then press Start. (If using fresh mozzarella cheese, set the cook time for 4 minutes.)

When the cooking time is up, use tongs to carefully transfer the chicken to a plate. Repeat to melt the cheese on the remaining chicken.

Top each breast with a few tablespoons of marinara sauce, garnish with basil leaves, and serve.

NOTE *Thin chicken breasts work best for this recipe. If your chicken breasts are very thick, cut them lengthwise horizontally before pounding (see step 1). Alternatively, you can purchase very thin chicken cutlets, which do not require pounding. The ideal thickness is ¼–½ inch (6–12 mm), allowing the chicken to be cooked through without drying out.*

VARIATION

Chicken Breast Sandwiches: *Prepare and cook the chicken breasts, omitting the marinara sauce and basil. To make sandwiches, place a chicken breast on the bottom half of an Italian-style roll or slice of Italian bread. Top with arugula, drizzle with balsamic vinegar and olive oil, sprinkle with freshly ground pepper, and cover with the top half of the roll or another bread slice. For a chicken Parmesan sandwich, omit the arugula, balsamic vinegar, and olive oil and top each chicken breast with a few tablespoons of marinara sauce.*

4 slices fresh or regular mozzarella cheese (each about ¼ inch/6 mm thick)

1 cup (240 ml) Marinara Sauce (page 135)

Fresh basil or flat-leaf parsley leaves, for garnish

Salt & Pepper Whole Roast Chicken

A combination of pressure cooking and broiling produces an incredibly juicy "roast" chicken. Pressure cook for 5 minutes per pound, then broil for an additional 30 minutes and in under an hour, you'll feast on a succulent bird that you'd swear emerged from an oven. Before getting started, be sure your chicken fits in the air fryer basket—4 lb (1.8 kg) or less is ideal.

SERVES 4–6

Pat the chicken dry with paper towels. Place 1 lemon half, the thyme, and garlic in the cavity, then tie the legs together with kitchen twine.

Place the chicken, breast-side up, in the Instant Pot® air fryer basket. Rub the skin all over with the oil. Sprinkle 1 teaspoon each salt and pepper all over the chicken and rub gently to distribute the seasonings evenly over the skin. Pour the water into the pot, insert the basket, and lock the pressure-cooking lid in place. Turn the valve to Sealing, press the Pressure Cook button and set the cook time for 5 minutes per pound at high pressure (a 4-lb/1.8-kg chicken would cook for 20 minutes), then press Start.

When the cooking time is up, press the Quick Release Button or turn the valve to Venting to quick-release the steam. Carefully remove the lid and press the Cancel button to reset the program. Use oven mitts to remove the basket from the pot and drain the water. Coat the chicken with olive oil spray and sprinkle the top of the chicken with ¼ teaspoon each salt and pepper. Insert the basket into the pot and attach the air fryer lid. Press the Broil button and set the cook time for 30 minutes at 400°F (200°C), then press Start. Cook undisturbed.

When the cooking time is up, insert an instant-read thermometer into a meaty part of the leg, away from the bone; it should register 165°F (74°C). If the chicken is not fully cooked, add more cooking time in 2-minute intervals. Wearing oven mitts, grab the legs with one hand, slowly lift the chicken out of the basket, and transfer to a cutting board. Cover loosely with aluminum foil and let rest for 10–15 minutes, then carve. Cut the remaining lemon half into wedges and serve alongside.

1 whole chicken (3–4 lb/ 1.4–1.8 kg) (see note)

1 lemon, cut in half

3 fresh thyme or rosemary sprigs

4 cloves garlic

2 tablespoons olive oil

Kosher salt and freshly ground black pepper

1½ cups (350 ml) water

This versatile comfort food is also delicious as a meatball sandwich or atop a big bowl of spaghetti squash.

Classic Turkey Meatballs

Packed with flavor, these meatballs are soft and pillowy thanks to dark turkey meat, ricotta cheese, and tomato paste. You can substitute chicken for the turkey, preferably dark meat as well, and enjoy either version over pasta with a classic marinara sauce.

SERVES 4

Line a rimmed baking sheet with parchment paper. In a bowl, beat the egg. Add the garlic, ricotta, Parmesan, tomato paste, oregano, 1 teaspoon salt, and ¼ teaspoon pepper and mix to combine. Add the turkey and bread crumbs and mix gently with your hands or a wooden spoon until just combined (be careful not to overmix or the meat will become tough).

Line a rimmed baking sheet with parchment paper. Pour the oil into a small bowl. Use a large ice cream scoop about 2¼ inches (5.5 cm) in diameter or a ¼-cup (60-ml) measure to scoop the meat mixture into equal-size balls. Place on the prepared baking sheet. You should have about 10 meatballs. Coat your palms and fingertips lightly with the oil. Roll each ball between your palms until smooth and evenly rounded. (The meatballs should be well oiled and shiny.)

Coat the Instant Pot® air fryer basket with canola oil spray. Working in batches, arrange a single layer of meatballs in the basket, making sure they don't touch. Insert the basket into the pot and attach the air fryer lid. Press the Air Fry button and set the cook time for 10 minutes at 375°F (190°C), then press Start. Rotate the meatballs when prompted.

When the cooking time is up, use tongs to carefully transfer the meatballs to a plate. Alternatively, place on a baking sheet in a 250°F (120°C) oven to keep warm. Repeat to cook the remaining batches. Serve the meatballs on their own or, if desired, over pasta topped with marinara sauce (page 135).

1 large egg

2 cloves garlic, minced or grated

2 tablespoons whole-milk ricotta cheese

2 tablespoons freshly grated Parmesan cheese

1 tablespoon tomato paste

1 teaspoon dried oregano

Kosher salt and freshly ground black pepper

1 lb (450 g) ground turkey (preferably dark meat)

¼ cup (¾ oz/25 g) panko bread crumbs

1 tablespoon olive oil

Southwestern Turkey Burgers with Corn Relish

For these mouthwatering burgers, the cheese is cooked inside the meat to help it stay moist. (But no one will stop you from sprinkling more on top, if you like.)

SERVES 4

In a bowl, stir together the bread crumbs, lime zest and juice, cumin, cayenne, and ¾ teaspoon salt. Add the turkey and mix gently with your hands or a wooden spoon until just combined (be careful not to overmix or the meat will become tough). Add the cheese and mix gently until just combined, making sure the cheese is evenly distributed. Divide the meat mixture into 4 equal-size balls, then shape into patties, each about 3½ inches (9 cm) in diameter and 1 inch (2.5 cm) thick. Cover and refrigerate for at least 30 minutes or up to 5 hours.

Meanwhile, make the corn relish: Select Sauté on the Instant Pot®, press Start, and heat the oil. Add the corn and bell pepper and cook, stirring constantly, until the vegetables are softened, about 3 minutes. Add the onion and garlic and cook, stirring occasionally, until the onion is softened, about 2 minutes. Stir in ⅛ teaspoon each salt and black pepper. Press the Cancel button to reset the program. Transfer the relish to a bowl and stir in the lime juice, cilantro, and jalapeño (if using). Taste and adjust the seasoning with salt and black pepper. Set aside. Grasp a paper towel with tongs and wipe out the pot; be careful, it will be hot.

Rub the patties on all sides with the oil. Use your thumb to make an indentation in the center of the each patty (this will prevent them from puffing up during cooking). Working with 2 at a time, arrange a single layer of patties in the air fryer basket, making sure they don't touch. Insert the basket into the pot and attach the air fryer lid. Press the Air Fry button and set the cook time for 15 minutes at 375°F (190°C), then press Start. Flip the burgers when prompted.

¼ cup (¾ oz/25 g) panko bread crumbs

1½ teaspoons grated lime zest

1½ teaspoons fresh lime juice

1 teaspoon ground cumin

⅛ teaspoon cayenne pepper, plus more if desired

Kosher salt

1 lb (450 g) ground turkey (preferably dark meat)

½ cup (4 oz/115 g) shredded pepper jack or Monterey jack cheese

A fresh corn and red bell pepper relish packs the sandwiches with even more punch and would be equally at home atop fish tacos (page 91) or salmon tacos (page 92).

When the cooking time is up, insert an instant-read thermometer into the center of a burger; it should register 165°F (74°C). If the burgers are not fully cooked, add more cooking time in 2-minute intervals until the burgers are fully cooked. (It's okay if a little cheese oozes out during cooking.) Use a nonstick spatula to carefully transfer the burgers to a plate. Alternatively, place on a baking sheet in a 250°F (120°C) oven to keep warm. Repeat to cook the remaining batches.

Place the burgers on the buns, top with a few generous spoonfuls of the corn relish and serve.

TIP *If you'd like to toast the buns, place 1 bun at a time, cut-sides down, on the dehydrating tray, insert the tray into the basket, and attach the air fryer lid. Press the Air Fry button and set the cook time for 2 minutes at 400°F (200°C), then press Start. When the cooking time is up, use tongs to transfer the bun to a plate. Repeat to toast the remaining bun.*

FOR THE CORN RELISH

2 teaspoons olive oil

1 cup (6 oz/170 g) fresh or thawed frozen corn kernels (from about 2 ears)

1 red bell pepper, seeded and chopped

6 tablespoons finely chopped red onion

1 teaspoon minced garlic

Kosher salt and freshly ground black pepper

1½ tablespoons fresh lime juice

1½ tablespoons chopped fresh cilantro

1 jalapeño chile, seeded and chopped (optional)

2 teaspoons olive oil

4 pretzel or brioche buns (page 118 or store-bought)

Pretzel-Crusted Chicken Tenders with Honey-Mustard Sauce

Almost any crushed, crunchy snack can stand in for bread crumbs (think cornflakes, potato chips, or corn chips). When crushing the topping, leave a few bigger pieces in the bag—the smaller ones will fill in all the nooks and crannies and the larger bits will provide texture.

SERVES 2

Place the pretzels in a large lock-top plastic bag and seal the bag. Using a rolling pin, meat pounder, or hammer, crush the pretzels until fine crumbs form (it's okay if a few larger chunks remain).

In a medium bowl, whisk together the flour, 1 teaspoon salt, and ¼ teaspoon pepper. In a large, shallow bowl, whisk together the egg, mustard, and water. Place the pretzel crumbs in another medium bowl or on a large plate.

Line a rimmed baking sheet with parchment paper. Pat the chicken dry with paper towels. Working with a few tenders at a time, coat the chicken in the flour mixture, shaking off the excess. Dip in the egg mixture, letting the excess drip off, then dredge in the pretzel mixture, turning to coat well and pressing gently to adhere. Place the coated chicken on the prepared baking sheet as you go.

Coat the Instant Pot® air fryer basket with canola oil spray. Working in batches, coat the chicken generously with canola oil spray and arrange a single layer of tenders in the basket, making sure they don't touch. Insert the basket into the pot and attach the air fryer lid. Press the Air Fry button and set the cook time for 10 minutes at 400°F (200°C), then press Start. Flip the chicken when prompted and spray both sides again with oil.

Meanwhile, make the honey-mustard sauce: In a small bowl, whisk together the honey, mustard, and a pinch of pepper. Taste and adjust the seasoning with more honey, mustard, or pepper.

When the cooking time is up, use tongs to transfer the chicken to a plate. Repeat to cook the remaining batches. Serve with the honey-mustard sauce alongside for dipping.

¼ lb (115 g) salted pretzels

¼ cup (1 oz/30 g) all-purpose flour

Kosher salt and freshly ground black pepper

1 large egg

1½ teaspoons Dijon mustard

1 teaspoon water

1 lb (450 g) chicken tenders

FOR THE HONEY-MUSTARD SAUCE

2 tablespoons honey, plus more as needed

2 tablespoons Dijon mustard, plus more as needed

Freshly ground black pepper

Chicken BLT

Wrapping chicken breasts in strips of bacon infuses the meat with flavor and also keeps it from drying out in the air fryer. Cut very thick chicken breasts in half horizontally or add more cooking time. Use country-style bread and toast it on the dehydrating tray just before assembling the sandwiches.

SERVES 2

Pat the chicken dry with paper towels. Season lightly with salt and pepper.

Wrap 2 bacon slices around each chicken breast, slightly overlapping the bacon so it covers as much surface area of the chicken as possible. Tuck the ends of the bacon underneath the slices so they stay in place when cooking. (Be sure the ends of both bacon slices are on the same side of the chicken so there is only 1 seam.)

Coat the Instant Pot® air fryer basket with canola oil spray. Place the chicken, seam-side down, in a single layer in the basket, making sure they don't touch. Insert the basket into the pot and attach the air fryer lid. Press the Air Fry button and set the cook time for 12 minutes at 400°F (200°C), then press Start. Cook undisturbed.

When the cooking time is up, insert an instant-read thermometer into the thickest part of the chicken; it should register 165°F (74°C). If the chicken is not fully cooked, add more cooking time in 2-minute intervals until the breasts are fully cooked. Use tongs to carefully transfer the chicken to a plate.

Place 2 bread slices on the dehydrating tray, insert the tray into the basket, and attach the air fryer lid. Press the Air Fry button and set the cook time for 2 minutes at 400°F (200°C), then press Start. When the cooking time is up, use tongs to transfer the bread to a plate. Repeat to toast the remaining bread slices.

For each sandwich, place 1 bread slice on a plate, spread evenly with mayo (if using), and place a chicken breast on the bread. Top with a lettuce leaf and 2 tomato slices, cover with another bread slice, and serve.

2 boneless, skinless chicken breasts (each about 6 oz/170 g) (see note)

Kosher salt and freshly ground black pepper

4 slices bacon

4 slices thick country bread, such as sourdough

Regular or Spicy Mayo (page 69), for serving (optional)

2 large romaine lettuce leaves

4 thick tomato slices

BBQ Chicken Drumsticks

Use either homemade or store-bought barbecue sauce for this versatile dish that's reminiscent of childhood summers. Budget-friendly drumsticks are often sold in family-size packages, so you can cook enough to feed a crowd. The Broil mode doesn't prompt you to turn food, so set a timer to alert you to brush on the sauce.

SERVES 2–3

Pat the chicken dry with paper towels. Using a small, sharp knife, poke a few holes in the skin (this will allow room for the skin to expand during cooking). Rub the chicken with the oil and season generously with salt and black pepper.

Coat the Instant Pot® air fryer basket with canola oil spray. Working in batches, arrange a single layer of drumsticks in the basket, making sure they don't touch. Insert the basket into the pot and attach the air fryer lid. Press the Broil button and set the cook time for 25 minutes at 400°F (200°C), then press Start. Set a separate timer for 19 minutes, at which point you will add the BBQ sauce.

Meanwhile, make the BBQ sauce: In a small saucepan over medium-low heat, whisk together the ketchup, vinegar, brown sugar, paprika, granulated garlic, chili powder, 1 teaspoon salt, and cayenne (if using). Bring to a simmer and cook, stirring occasionally, until the sauce is slightly reduced and darkened in color, about 10 minutes.

Six minutes before the chicken has finished cooking, remove the air fryer lid and brush the drumsticks generously all over with some of the BBQ sauce. (It might be easiest to transfer the drumsticks to a plate to coat them evenly.) Attach the lid and continue the cooking program.

When the cooking time is up, insert an instant-read thermometer into the center of a drumstick, away from the bone; it should register 165°F (74°C). If the chicken is not fully cooked, add more cooking time in 2-minute intervals. Use tongs to carefully transfer the chicken to a plate. Repeat to cook the remaining batches. Serve the chicken with the remaining BBQ sauce alongside.

2 lb (1 kg) chicken drumsticks (about 6)

2 teaspoons canola oil

Kosher salt and freshly ground black pepper

FOR THE BBQ SAUCE

⅔ cup (5½ oz/155 g) ketchup

½ cup (120 ml) apple cider vinegar

⅓ cup (2¾ oz/80 g) firmly packed light brown sugar

2 teaspoons smoked paprika

2 teaspoons granulated garlic

1 teaspoon chili powder

Kosher salt

Pinch of cayenne pepper (optional)

Five-Spice Chicken Thighs

An aromatic blend that includes soy sauce, brown sugar, toasted sesame oil, ginger, garlic, and Chinese five-spice powder adds irresistible flavor and keeps these chicken thighs moist while cooking. As the sugar caramelizes, things can get a little messy in the pot, and the corners of the skin will become dark and crispy, making that first bite taste even better.

SERVES 4

Pat the chicken dry with paper towels. Using a small, sharp knife, poke a few holes in the skin (this will allow room for the skin to expand during cooking). Season the chicken lightly with salt and let stand at room temperature for 30 minutes.

Meanwhile, in a large glass measuring cup or medium bowl, whisk together the soy sauce, mirin, brown sugar, sesame oil, ginger, garlic, and five-spice powder. Place the chicken in a large lock-top plastic bag and pour in the marinade. Seal the bag, massaging the marinade around the chicken. Refrigerate for at least 4 hours or up to overnight, turning the bag over several times while the chicken is marinating.

Coat the Instant Pot® air fryer basket with canola oil spray or line it with parchment paper cut to fit. Working in batches, remove the chicken from the marinade, letting the excess drip off, and arrange a single layer of thighs in the basket, making sure they don't touch. Insert the basket into the pot and attach the air fryer lid. Press the Air Fry button and set the cook time for 17 minutes at 325°F (165°C), then press Start. Cook undisturbed.

When the cooking time is up, insert an instant-read thermometer into the center of a thigh, away from the bone; it should register 175°F (80°C). If the chicken is not fully cooked, add more cooking time in 2-minute intervals until the thighs are fully cooked. Use tongs to carefully transfer the chicken to a plate. Alternatively, place on a baking sheet in a 250°F (120°C) oven to keep warm. Repeat to cook the remaining batches, then serve.

2 lb (1 kg) bone-in, skin-on chicken thighs

Kosher salt

¼ cup (60 ml) soy sauce

¼ cup (60 ml) mirin

¼ cup (2 oz/60 g) firmly packed light brown sugar

2 teaspoons toasted sesame oil

2 teaspoons peeled and grated fresh ginger

3 cloves garlic, grated

1 teaspoon Chinese five-spice powder

Honey-Glazed Chicken Leg Quarters

Chicken cooked on the Broil setting turns out amazingly juicy. By adding a sweet and slightly spicy glaze near the end of cooking, the honey caramelizes nicely but doesn't burn. Brushing the legs again with glaze when they're done seals in the flavor even more. Fish sauce lends umami to the glaze, but you can skip it if you prefer.

SERVES 2

Pat the chicken dry with paper towels. Using a small, sharp knife, poke a few holes in the skin (this will allow room for the skin to expand during cooking). Rub each chicken leg with 1 teaspoon of the oil and season generously with salt and pepper.

Coat the Instant Pot® air fryer basket with canola oil spray. Arrange the chicken legs in a single layer in the basket, making sure they don't touch (if the legs are very large, only 1 might fit at a time). Insert the basket into the pot and attach the air fryer lid. Press the Broil button and set the cook time for 25 minutes at 400°F (200°C), then press Start. Set a separate timer for 17 minutes, at which point you will add the glaze.

Meanwhile, make the honey glaze: In a small bowl, whisk together the honey, Sriracha, and fish sauce. Set aside.

Eight minutes before the chicken has finished cooking, remove the air fryer lid and brush the legs generously all over with some of the glaze. (It might be easiest to transfer the legs to a plate to coat them evenly.) Attach the lid and continue the cooking program.

When the cooking time is up, insert an instant-read thermometer into the center of a leg, away from the bone; it should register 175°F (74°C). If the chicken is not fully cooked, add more cooking time in 2-minute intervals until the legs are fully cooked. Use tongs to carefully transfer the chicken to a plate, brush with more glaze, and serve.

2 full chicken leg quarters (thigh and drumstick attached) (about 1½ lb/680 g total)

2 teaspoons canola oil

Kosher salt and freshly ground black pepper

FOR THE HONEY GLAZE

3 tablespoons honey

1½ teaspoons Sriracha or other hot sauce

1 teaspoon fish sauce (see note)

Chicken Teriyaki Bowls

Skinless, unbreaded chicken needs a strong barrier to withstand the intense dry heat of the Instant Pot®, and this marinade does the trick. Be sure to coat the pieces well with canola oil spray, which helps the outside stay moist. Serve over a bowl of rice or rice noodles with your favorite veggies and toppings for a satisfying lunch or dinner.

SERVES 4

In a small bowl or glass measuring cup, whisk together the honey, soy sauce, vinegar, ginger, and garlic. Place the chicken in a large lock-top plastic bag or shallow baking dish. Pour the marinade over the chicken and toss well to coat. Seal the bag, massaging the marinade around the chicken, or cover the container. Refrigerate for at least 1 hour or up to 8 hours, turning the chicken occasionally.

Coat the Instant Pot® air fryer basket with canola oil spray. Working in batches, remove the chicken from the marinade, letting the excess drip off. Coat the chicken lightly with canola oil spray and arrange a single layer of pieces in the basket, making sure they don't touch. Insert the basket into the pot and attach the air fryer lid. Press the Air Fry button and set the cook time for 8 minutes at 350°F (180°C), then press Start. Flip the chicken when prompted.

Meanwhile, make the marinated cucumbers: In a medium bowl, whisk together the sake, sesame oil, and soy sauce. Add the cucumbers and toss to coat. Let stand while the chicken cooks, or for at least 15 minutes.

When the cooking time is up, use tongs to carefully transfer the chicken to a cutting board. Repeat to cook the remaining batches. When the chicken is cool enough to handle, cut into strips.

Divide the rice among 4 bowls. Drain the cucumbers and distribute them evenly over the rice. Top with the chicken and avocados. Drizzle with soy sauce and sesame oil, sprinkle with sesame seeds, and serve.

½ cup (6 oz/170 g) honey

¼ cup (60 ml) soy sauce

1 tablespoon rice vinegar

1 tablespoon peeled and chopped fresh ginger

2 cloves garlic, chopped

2 large boneless, skinless chicken breasts (1½–2 lb/ 680 g–1 kg total), cut lengthwise horizontally

FOR THE MARINATED CUCUMBERS
½ cup (120 ml) sake or mirin

3 tablespoons toasted sesame oil

1 tablespoon soy sauce

2 cucumbers, thinly sliced

FOR SERVING
Cooked rice (page 136)

2 avocados, pitted, peeled, and thinly sliced

Soy sauce

Toasted sesame oil

Toasted sesame seeds

Tandoori Chicken Tenders

An Indian-inspired yogurt marinade keeps these chicken strips exceptionally juicy after air frying and creates just the right amount of charred spots to mimic tandoori cooking. (Add more or less cayenne pepper to the marinade depending on your desired level of heat.) A tangy lemon-yogurt dip complements the spicy sauce.

SERVES 2–4

In a large bowl, stir together the yogurt, tomato paste, lemon juice, garam masala, turmeric, cayenne, 1 teaspoon salt, and a few grindings of black pepper. Add the chicken and toss to coat. Cover and refrigerate for at least 30 minutes or up to 1 hour.

Meanwhile, make the herbed lemon-yogurt dip: In a small bowl, stir together the yogurt, lemon zest and juice, and cilantro. Season to taste with salt and pepper. Cover and refrigerate until ready to use.

Line the Instant Pot® air fryer basket with an air fryer liner or parchment paper cut to fit and coat the liner with canola oil spray. Working in batches, remove the chicken from the marinade, letting the excess drip off. Coat the chicken lightly with canola oil spray and arrange a single layer of tenders in the basket, making sure they don't touch. Insert the basket into the pot and attach the air fryer lid. Press the Broil button and set the cook time for 10 minutes at 400°F (200°C), then press Start. Cook undisturbed.

When the cooking time is up, use tongs to carefully transfer the chicken to a plate. Alternatively, place on a baking sheet in a 250°F (120°C) oven to keep warm. Repeat to cook the remaining batches. Serve with the herbed lemon-yogurt dip and naan bread alongside, if desired.

¾ **cup (6 oz/170 g) plain whole-milk yogurt**

1 **tablespoon tomato paste**

1 **tablespoon fresh lemon juice**

2 **teaspoons garam masala**

1 **teaspoon ground turmeric**

⅛ **teaspoon or pinch of cayenne pepper**

Kosher salt and freshly ground black pepper

1–1½ **lb (450–680 g) chicken tenders**

FOR THE HERBED LEMON-YOGURT DIP
¾ **cup (6 oz/170 g) plain whole-milk yogurt**

Grated zest and juice of ½ lemon

1 **tablespoon chopped fresh cilantro**

Kosher salt and freshly ground black pepper

Naan bread, for serving (optional)

Parmesan-Crusted Halibut

Here, Parmesan cheese in the bread crumb mixture lends a sharp, nutty, savory flavor along with a little crunch—a wonderful complement to a silky fillet of fresh halibut. Spritzing a bit of olive oil on the breading mixture before coating the fish will help it to stick.

SERVES 2

Place the flour in a medium bowl. In a large, shallow bowl, whisk together the egg and water. In another medium bowl or on a large plate, stir together the bread crumbs, cheese, oregano, ½ teaspoon salt, and ¼ teaspoon pepper.

Line a rimmed baking sheet with parchment paper. Pat the halibut fillets dry with paper towels. Season generously with salt and pepper. Working with 1 fillet at a time, coat the fish in flour, shaking off the excess. Dip in the egg mixture, letting the excess drip off, then dredge in the bread crumb mixture, turning to coat well on all sides and pressing gently to adhere. Place the coated fillets on the prepared baking sheet as you go.

Make a foil sling for the Instant Pot® air fryer basket (see page 94)

Coat the fillets with olive oil spray and arrange them in a single layer on the sling, making sure they don't touch. (The ends of the fillets will hang over the foil and touch the basket.) Insert the basket into the pot and attach the air fryer lid. Press the Air Fry button and set the cook time for 8 minutes at 400°F (200°C), then press Start. Cook undisturbed.

When the cooking time is up, insert an instant-read thermometer into the thickest part of a fillet; it should register 130°–135°F (54°–57°C) for medium. If the halibut is not cooked to the desired doneness, add more cooking time in 1-minute intervals until the halibut is cooked as desired. Use a nonstick spatula to carefully transfer the halibut to a plate. Or, wearing oven mitts, carefully grab the foil sling on each end, lift it out of the basket, and transfer the halibut to a plate. Serve with lemon wedges and potatoes, if desired, alongside.

¼ cup (1 oz/30 g) all-purpose flour

1 large egg

1 teaspoon water

½ cup (1¾ oz/50 g) panko bread crumbs

½ cup (2 oz/60 g) freshly grated Parmesan cheese

½ teaspoon dried oregano

Kosher salt and freshly ground black pepper

2 halibut fillets (each 6–8 oz/ 170–225 g and 1–1½ inches/ 2.5–4 cm thick), skin removed

Lemon wedges, for serving

Classic Roast Potatoes or Herb-Roasted Potatoes (page 46), for serving (optional)

Coconut Shrimp

Unsweetened shredded coconut adds an amazing taste and texture to this healthier version of the popular fried seafood dish. Serve by itself as an appetizer or with coconut rice (page 137) and veggies as a main meal. Sweet chili sauce or duck sauce pairs well with the crunchy coating on the shrimp.

SERVES 4

In a bowl, whisk together the flour, 2 teaspoons salt, and ½ teaspoon pepper. In another bowl, whisk together the eggs and water. In a third bowl, stir together the coconut and bread crumbs.

Line a rimmed baking sheet with parchment paper. Pat the shrimp dry with paper towels. Working with a few shrimp at a time, toss them in the flour mixture, shaking off the excess. Dip in the egg mixture, letting the excess drip off, then dredge in the coconut mixture, pressing firmly to adhere. Place the coated shrimp on the prepared baking sheet as you go.

Coat the Instant Pot® air fryer basket with canola oil spray. Working in batches, arrange a single layer of shrimp in the basket, making sure they don't touch. Insert the basket into the pot and attach the air fryer lid. Press the Air Fry button and set the cook time for 8 minutes at 400°F (200°), then press Start. Flip the shrimp when prompted.

When the cooking time is up, use tongs to carefully transfer the shrimp to a plate. Repeat to cook the remaining batches. Serve with chili sauce or duck sauce alongside for dipping, if desired.

½ cup (2 oz/60 g) **all-purpose flour**

Kosher salt and freshly ground black pepper

2 large eggs

2 teaspoons water

⅔ cup (2½ oz/70 g) **unsweetened shredded coconut**

⅔ cup (2¼ oz/65 g) panko **bread crumbs**

1 lb (450 g) jumbo shrimp, **peeled and deveined**

Thai sweet chili sauce or duck sauce, for serving (optional)

Baja Fish Tacos

Lots of fresh toppings—lime crema, homemade pico de gallo, shredded cabbage, and cilantro—brighten up beer-battered fish fillets in these Mexican-inspired tacos. Warm the corn tortillas over an open flame on the stove for a few seconds for a charred effect.

SERVES 4

In a medium bowl, stir together the flour, cornstarch, 2 teaspoons salt, 1 teaspoon black pepper, granulated garlic, and cayenne. In another medium bowl, whisk together the egg and beer.

Set a wire rack on a rimmed baking sheet. Pat the fish dry with a paper towel. Cut into strips about 3 inches (7.5 cm) long and 1 inch (2.5 cm) wide. Working with a few strips at a time, coat the fish in the flour mixture, shaking off the excess. Dip in the egg mixture, letting the excess drip off. Return the fish to the flour mixture and coat well, shaking off the excess. Place the coated fish on the wire rack as you go.

Coat the Instant Pot® air fryer basket with canola oil spray. Working in batches, coat the fish strips generously with canola oil and arrange a single layer of strips in the basket, making sure they don't touch. Insert the basket into the pot and attach the air fryer lid. Press the Air Fry button and set the cook time for 15 minutes at 375°F (190°C), then press Start. Flip the fish strips when prompted, coating again with oil.

Meanwhile, make the lime crema: In a small bowl, stir together the sour cream, half the lime juice, ¼ teaspoon salt, and a few grindings of black pepper. Taste and adjust the seasoning as needed.

To make the pico de gallo, in a small bowl, stir together the tomatoes, onion, chile, cilantro, lime juice, and ½ teaspoon salt. Taste and adjust the seasoning as needed.

When the cooking time is up, use tongs to carefully transfer the fish to a plate and season to taste with salt and black pepper. Repeat to cook the remaining batches.

Spread some lime crema on the tortillas and top with the fish, cabbage, pico de gallo, and cilantro. Serve with lime wedges alongside.

¾ cup (3 oz/90 g) **all-purpose flour**

¾ cup (3 oz/90 g) cornstarch

Kosher salt and freshly ground black pepper

1 teaspoon granulated garlic

¼ **teaspoon cayenne pepper**

1 large egg

⅔ cup (150 ml) light beer

1 lb (450 g) firm, skinless white fish, such as cod

FOR THE LIME CREMA
1 cup (8 oz/225 g) sour cream

Juice of 1 lime

FOR THE PICO DE GALLO
2 plum tomatoes, seeded and diced

¼ **white onion, diced**

1 serrano or jalapeño chile, seeded, if desired, and minced

2 tablespoons finely chopped fresh cilantro

1 tablespoon fresh lime juice, plus more as needed

Corn tortillas, shredded cabbage, cilantro, and lime wedges, for serving

Spice-Rubbed Salmon Tacos with Crispy Slaw

This kid-friendly dinner is sure to become a staple in your household. Young chefs can lend a hand by mixing up the slaw and lime crema. Set out all the ingredients in separate bowls and plates, then let everyone assemble their own tacos as they please. Enjoy any leftover salmon on a salad or rice bowl for lunch the next day.

SERVES 4

To make the spice rub, in a small bowl, stir together the ancho chile powder, cumin, coriander, ½ teaspoon salt, and ¼ teaspoon pepper. Rub the salmon all over with the oil and sprinkle the spice mixture over the non-skin side of the salmon.

Make a foil sling for the Instant Pot® air fryer basket (see page 94).

Place the salmon, skin-side down, on the sling. (The ends of the salmon will hang over the foil and touch the basket.) Insert the basket into the pot and attach the air fryer lid. Press the Broil button and set the cook time for 10 minutes at 400°F (200°C), then press Start. Cook undisturbed.

Meanwhile, make the crispy slaw: In a medium bowl, stir together the cabbage, cilantro, lime juice, chile, and ½ teaspoon salt. Taste and adjust the seasoning with salt. Set aside.

When the cooking time is up, insert an instant-read thermometer into the center of the thickest part of the salmon; it should register 120°–125°F (49°–52°C) for medium-rare. If the salmon is not cooked to the desired doneness, add more cooking time in 1-minute intervals if needed until the salmon is cooked as desired. Wearing oven mitts, carefully grab the foil sling on each end, lift it out of the basket, and transfer the salmon to a plate.

Shred the salmon with a fork and divide it among the tortillas. Top with the slaw, drizzle with lime crema, and sprinkle with cilantro. Serve with lime wedges alongside.

FOR THE SPICE RUB
¾ teaspoon ancho chile powder

¼ teaspoon ground cumin

¼ teaspoon ground coriander

Kosher salt and freshly ground black pepper

1 lb (450 g) salmon, skin on

1 teaspoon olive oil

FOR THE CRISPY SLAW
1 cup (3 oz/90 g) shredded cabbage (red, green, or a combination)

¼ cup (¼ oz/7 g) fresh cilantro leaves, chopped

2 tablespoons fresh lime juice

1 serrano chile, seeded, if desired, and minced

Kosher salt

FOR SERVING
8 corn tortillas, warmed

Lime Crema (page 91), fresh cilantro leaves, lime wedges

Crispy Crab Cakes with Tartar Sauce

Fresh cooked lump crabmeat will yield the best flavor and texture, which is well balanced by a crisp coating of panko bread crumbs. Serve these crab cakes with homemade or store-bought tartar sauce by themselves, atop a bed of mixed greens, or nestled in a brioche bun (page 118) for a fantastic sandwich.

SERVES 4

Line a rimmed baking sheet with parchment paper. Place the crabmeat in a medium bowl and season generously with salt and pepper. Add the eggs, mustard, Worcestershire sauce, garlic, and dill and mix with a rubber spatula until just combined. Add the crushed crackers and mix gently to combine. Divide the mixture into 4 equal portions, then shape into patties, each about 3 inches (7.5 cm) in diameter and 1 inch (2.5 cm) thick. Place on the prepared baking sheet, cover with plastic wrap, and refrigerate for 30 minutes.

Meanwhile, make the tartar sauce: In a small bowl, stir together the mayonnaise, cornichons, tarragon, lemon juice, and mustard. Season to taste with salt and pepper. Stir in water 1 teaspoon at a time to reach the desired consistency. Cover and refrigerate until ready to use.

Place the bread crumbs on a large plate and spritz lightly with olive oil spray. (This will help the crumbs stick to the crab cakes.) Working with 1 crab cake at a time, dredge in the crumbs, coating all sides, and return to the baking sheet.

Coat the Instant Pot® air fryer basket with canola oil spray. Working with 2 at a time, coat the crab cakes with olive oil spray and arrange a single layer of crab cakes in the basket, making sure they don't touch. Insert the basket into the pot and attach the air fryer lid. Press the Air Fry button and set the cook time for 16 minutes at 350°F (180°C), then press Start. Carefully flip the crab cakes when prompted.

When the cooking time is up, use a nonstick spatula to carefully transfer the crab cakes to a plate. Repeat to cook the remaining batches. Serve with the tartar sauce and lemon wedges alongside.

½ lb (225 g) cooked crabmeat, preferably lump

Kosher salt and freshly ground black pepper

2 large eggs, lightly beaten

1 tablespoon Dijon mustard

1 tablespoon Worcestershire sauce

2 cloves garlic, minced

¼ cup (½ oz/15 g) chopped fresh dill

1 cup (3½ oz/100 g) crushed saltine crackers (about 16 crackers)

FOR THE TARTAR SAUCE
1 cup (240 ml) mayonnaise

2 tablespoons chopped cornichons

1 tablespoon minced fresh tarragon

1 tablespoon fresh lemon juice

1 teaspoon Dijon mustard

Kosher salt and freshly ground black pepper

1 cup (3½ oz/100 g) panko bread crumbs

Lemon wedges, for serving

Ginger-Soy Salmon

A foil sling prevents the salmon from sticking to the air fryer basket and makes easy work of removing the delicate fish from the pot. If your fillets are thicker or weigh more than the measurements indicated below, broil them a few minutes longer until they reach the desired doneness.

SERVES 2

In a small bowl, whisk together the soy sauce, brown sugar, lime juice, sesame oil, ginger, and garlic. Place the salmon fillets in a shallow baking dish just large enough to hold them and pour the marinade over the fish. Cover with plastic wrap and refrigerate for at least 30 minutes or up to 2 hours, turning occasionally.

Make a foil sling for the Instant Pot® air fryer basket by folding a sheet of aluminum foil into a strip about 4 inches (10 cm) wide by 20 inches (50 cm) long. Lay the strip of foil across the center of the basket, pressing it into and up the sides. Fold any excess foil over the top edges of the basket. Coat the basket and foil with canola oil spray.

Remove the salmon from the marinade, letting the excess drip off. Arrange the fillets, skin-side down, in a single layer on the sling, making sure they don't touch. (The ends of the fillets will hang over the foil and touch the basket.) Insert the basket into the pot and attach the air fryer lid. Press the Broil button and set the cook time for 7 minutes at 400°F (200°C), then press Start. Cook undisturbed.

When the cooking time is up, insert an instant-read thermometer into the center of the thickest part of a fillet; it should register 120°–125°F (49°–52°C) for medium-rare. If the salmon is not cooked to the desired doneness, add more cooking time in 1-minute intervals until the salmon is cooked as desired. Use a nonstick spatula to carefully transfer the salmon to a plate. Or, wearing oven mitts, carefully grab the foil sling on each end, lift it out of the basket, and transfer the salmon to a plate. Serve with rice alongside, if desired.

¼ **cup (60 ml) soy sauce**

3 tablespoons firmly packed light brown sugar

2 tablespoons fresh lime juice

1 tablespoon toasted sesame oil

1 tablespoon peeled and grated fresh ginger

2 cloves garlic, grated

2 salmon fillets (each 6–8 oz/170–225 g and 1–1½ inches/2.5–4 cm thick), skin on

Steamed rice, for serving (page 136) (optional)

Leftover salmon is the perfect addition to a lunchtime salad or rice bowl.

Crispy Tofu with Sesame-Soy-Ginger Sauce

Achieving a crisp exterior on tofu can be a challenge because of its moist texture. By drying the tofu block well before cooking and coating the cubes with canola oil spray, the results are flawless after air frying. This dish is a great match with green beans—try the recipe on page 49, omitting the Old Bay seasoning.

SERVES 4–6

Set a wire rack on a rimmed baking sheet. Place the tofu on the rack and cover with several layers of paper towels. Top with a heavy pot to weigh down the tofu and drain the excess water. Let stand for 30 minutes.

Meanwhile, make the sesame-soy-ginger sauce: In a small bowl or glass measuring cup, whisk together the oil, soy sauce, vinegar, ginger, garlic, honey, red pepper flakes, green onions, and ¼ teaspoon salt. Set aside.

Coat the Instant Pot® air fryer basket with canola oil spray. Cut the tofu into 1-inch (2.5-cm) cubes. Working in batches, coat the tofu cubes with canola oil spray and arrange a single layer of cubes in the basket, making sure they don't touch. Insert the basket into the pot and attach the air fryer lid. Press the Air Fry button and set the cook time for 12 minutes at 400°F (200°C), then press Start. Flip the tofu when prompted.

When the cooking time is up, use tongs to carefully transfer the tofu to a plate. Repeat to cook the remaining batches.

Place the rice (if using) in a serving bowl and top with the tofu. Pour the sauce over the tofu, sprinkle with sesame seeds, and serve.

14 oz (400 g) extra-firm tofu

FOR THE SESAME-SOY-GINGER SAUCE

3 tablespoons toasted sesame oil

3 tablespoons soy sauce

2 tablespoons rice vinegar

2 teaspoons peeled and minced or grated fresh ginger

1 clove garlic, minced or grated

2 teaspoons honey

¼ teaspoon red pepper flakes

¼ cup (¾ oz/20 g) thinly sliced green onions, white and pale green parts

Kosher salt

Cooked rice (page 136), for serving (optional)

Toasted sesame seeds, for serving

Eggplant Parmesan

This simple take on a classic Italian meal makes for a satisfying main dish or as a complement alongside turkey meatballs (page 77). The dehydrating tray melts the cheese on the breaded eggplant rounds in no time. If your eggplant is larger than 1 lb (450 g), you may need to add more crumbs to the breading mixture.

SERVES 4

Place the eggplant slices in a single layer on a plate or rimmed baking sheet and sprinkle with ¾ teaspoon salt. Let stand for 15 minutes. Using paper towels, gently blot the eggplant to remove excess moisture.

In a bowl, whisk together the eggs and water. In another bowl, stir together the bread crumbs, Parmesan, and a few grindings of pepper.

Working with 1 slice at a time, dip the eggplant in the egg mixture, letting the excess drip off. Dredge in the bread crumb mixture.

Coat the Instant Pot® air fryer basket with canola oil spray. Working in batches, coat the eggplant slices on both sides with olive oil spray and arrange a single layer of slices in the basket, making sure they don't touch. Insert the basket into the pot and attach the air fryer lid. Press the Air Fry button and set the cook time for 7 minutes at 400°F (200°C), then press Start. Flip the eggplant when prompted.

When the cooking time is up, use tongs to carefully transfer the eggplant to a plate. Repeat to cook the remaining batches.

Insert the dehydrating tray into the air fryer basket. Working in batches, arrange a single layer of eggplant slices on the tray. Lay 1 piece of mozzarella cheese on top of each eggplant slice. Attach the air fryer lid. Press the Broil button and set the cook time for 3 minutes at 400°F (200°C), then press Start. (If using fresh mozzarella cheese, set the cook time for 4 minutes.)

When the cooking time is up, use a nonstick spatula or tongs to transfer the eggplant to a plate. Top each eggplant slice with a dollop of marinara sauce, sprinkle with Parmesan and parsley, and serve.

1 large eggplant (about 1 lb/ 450 g), cut crosswise into slices ½ inch (12 mm) thick

Kosher salt and freshly ground black pepper

2 large eggs

1 teaspoon water

1 cup (3½ oz/100 g) plain dried Italian bread crumbs

3 tablespoons freshly grated Parmesan cheese, plus more for serving

½ lb (225 g) fresh or regular mozzarella cheese, cut into slices ¼ inch (6 mm) thick

1 cup (240 ml) Marinara Sauce (page 135)

Chopped fresh flat-leaf parsley, for serving

Veggie Frittata

This versatile baked egg dish works well with almost any combination of vegetables and herbs—use what you have on hand and design your own. You can swap the Swiss chard for kale or spinach, substitute any summer squash for the zucchini, and choose whatever fresh herbs you like. Leftover slices are great for a portable breakfast on the go.

SERVES 6

Grease a 1½-qt (1.4-L) round ceramic baking dish with butter or coat with canola oil spray. In a large bowl, whisk together the eggs, milk, ½ teaspoon salt, and ¼ teaspoon pepper. Set aside.

Select Sauté on the Instant Pot®, press Start, and heat the oil. Add the shallot and cook, stirring occasionally, until just softened, about 1 minute. Add the chard and ¼ teaspoon salt and cook, until the chard starts to soften, about 3 minutes. Move the chard to one side of the pot and add the mushrooms to the empty side. Cook until the mushrooms start to brown and release some of their liquid, about 2 minutes. Move the mushrooms to the side of the pot with the chard and add the zucchini to the empty side. Cook until the zucchini starts to soften, about 2 minutes. Stir the chard, mushrooms, and zucchini together and cook for 1 minute longer to evaporate any excess liquid. Press the Cancel button to reset the program.

Transfer the vegetable mixture to the egg mixture and stir to combine. Fold in the tomatoes, herbs, and cheese. Pour into the prepared baking dish. Wipe or rinse out the pot. Place the baking dish on the steam rack. Using the handles, lower the baking dish and steam rack into the pot and attach the air fryer lid. Press the Air Fry button and set the cook time for 25 minutes at 300°F (150°C), then press Start. Cook undisturbed.

When the cooking time is up, use a toothpick to check if the eggs are set. If the frittata is still very wobbly and wet inside, add more cooking time in 2-minute intervals until the eggs are set. Using the steam rack handles, lift out the baking dish. Let the frittata cool slightly before cutting it into wedges and serving.

6 large eggs

½ cup (120 ml) whole milk

Kosher salt and freshly ground black pepper

1 tablespoon canola or avocado oil

1 large shallot, thinly sliced

¼ lb (115 g) Swiss chard, thick stems and ribs removed, leaves chopped

¼ lb (115 g) cremini or baby bella mushrooms, brushed clean and sliced

1 zucchini, thinly sliced

⅓ cup (2 oz/60 g) halved grape or cherry tomatoes

1 tablespoon chopped fresh flat-leaf parsley, dill, chives, or any combination

1 cup (4 oz/115 g) shredded white Cheddar or mozzarella cheese

Falafel Pita Sandwiches

If you've been reluctant to prepare falafel at home because of all the fuss involved with frying, this recipe is for you. Soak dried chickpeas overnight so they become just soft enough to grind in a food processor,

SERVES 6 (MAKES 12 FALAFEL BALLS)

In a food processor, combine the chickpeas, shallots, garlic, parsley, and cilantro and process until finely chopped. Add the cumin, coriander, paprika, cayenne, 2 tablespoons of the oil, 1½ teaspoons salt, and a few grindings of black pepper and process until blended. (The mixture should have an even consistency but should not be completely smooth.)

Line a rimmed baking sheet with parchment paper. Pour the remaining 1 tablespoon oil into a small bowl. Use a large ice cream scoop about 2 inches (5 cm) in diameter or a tablespoon measure to scoop the chickpea mixture into equal-size balls, each about 3 tablespoons. Place on the prepared baking sheet. Coat your palms and fingertips lightly with the oil. Roll each ball between your palms until smooth and evenly rounded.

Coat the Instant Pot® air fryer basket with canola oil spray. Working in batches, arrange a single layer of chickpea balls in the basket, making sure they don't touch. Insert the basket into the pot and attach the air fryer lid. Press the Air Fry button and set the cook time for 15 minutes at 400°F (200°C), then press Start. Rotate the balls when prompted.

Meanwhile, make the lemon-yogurt sauce: In a small bowl, stir together the yogurt, lemon juice, and dill. Season to taste with salt and black pepper. Set aside.

2 cups (14 oz/400 g) dried chickpeas, rinsed and picked over, soaked overnight, and drained

2 shallots, halved

3 cloves garlic

¼ cup (¼ oz/7 g) fresh flat-leaf parsley leaves

¼ cup (¼ oz/7 g) fresh cilantro leaves

2 teaspoons ground cumin

2 teaspoons ground coriander

2 teaspoons smoked paprika

¼ teaspoon cayenne pepper

3 tablespoons olive oil, plus more for drizzling

Kosher salt and freshly ground black pepper

then blend in a good amount of aromatics, herbs, and spices and a little olive oil and you have falafel batter in minutes. These balls are equally delicious tucked inside a pita sandwich or served over a fresh green salad.

When the cooking time is up, use tongs to carefully transfer the falafel to a plate. Drizzle with oil and sprinkle with a little salt. Repeat to cook the remaining batches.

Warm the pita breads, if desired (see tip), and cut them in half. For each sandwich, cut a falafel in half and place inside a pita half, then add lettuce leaves and tomato slices. Drizzle with the lemon-yogurt sauce and serve.

TIP *You can warm the pita breads on the dehydrating tray set in the air fryer basket. Place 1 or 2 breads at a time on the tray, insert the basket into the pot, and attach the air fryer lid. Press the Air Fry button and set the cook time for 2 minutes at 400°F (200°C), then press Start.*

VARIATION

Falafel Salad: *To make individual falafel salads, assemble and cook the falafel as directed above. Chop the lettuce and place in a bowl. Top each salad with 2 falafel balls, a few tomato slices, and any other vegetables you like, such as thinly sliced cucumbers, carrots, radishes, and celery. Make the lemon-yogurt sauce as directed, adding more lemon juice, if desired, for a thinner consistency. Drizzle the sauce over the salad and sprinkle with chopped dill and a few grindings of pepper.*

FOR THE LEMON-YOGURT SAUCE
½ cup (4 oz/115 g) plain whole-milk yogurt

1 tablespoon fresh lemon juice

1 teaspoon chopped fresh dill

Kosher salt and freshly ground black pepper

FOR SERVING
Pita breads, lettuce leaves, tomato slices

Mini Berry Hand Pies
(page 110)

SWEET TREATS

Lemon–Poppy Seed Drizzle Cake

The combination of lemon and poppy seeds is a match made in heaven. Add them both to a buttery cake batter and you'll create dessert perfection. Fresh lemon juice lends just the right amount of tartness to the glaze, which finishes the cake with a sweet flourish.

SERVES 6–8

Grease an 8-inch (20-cm) Bundt pan with butter or coat with canola oil spray. In a bowl, whisk together the flour, poppy seeds, baking powder, and salt. Set aside.

In the bowl of a stand mixer fitted with the paddle attachment, beat together the butter, granulated sugar, and lemon zest on medium-high speed until light and fluffy, 3–5 minutes. Stop the mixer and scrape down the sides of the bowl with a rubber spatula. Add the eggs one at a time, beating well on medium speed after each addition. Add the sour cream and vanilla and beat until combined, about 2 minutes. (The batter will form ribbons at this stage.) Stop the mixer and scrape down the sides of the bowl. Add the flour mixture and beat on low speed until just combined, about 1 minute. Pour the batter into the prepared pan.

Place the Bundt pan on the steam rack. Using the handles, lower the pan and the steam rack into the Instant Pot® and attach the air fryer lid. Press the Bake button and set the cook time for 30 minutes at 325°F (165°C), then press Start. Bake undisturbed.

When the cooking time is up, use a toothpick to check if the cake is cooked all the way through; it should come out clean or with a few loose crumbs attached. If not, add more cooking time in 2-minute intervals until the cake is cooked through. Using the steam rack handles, lift out the pan and transfer it to a wire rack until cool enough to handle. Remove the cake from the pan and return it to the wire rack. Set the wire rack on a baking sheet.

To make the glaze, in a glass measuring cup, stir together the confectioners' sugar and lemon juice until the sugar has dissolved. Pour the glaze in a circle over the top of the cake, letting it drip down along the outer edges of the cake. Sprinkle the top with poppy seeds. Cut the cake into wedges and serve.

1½ cups (6½ oz/185 g) all-purpose flour

1 tablespoon poppy seeds, plus more for sprinkling

1 teaspoon baking powder

½ teaspoon kosher salt

¾ cup (6 oz/170 g) unsalted butter, at room temperature, plus more for greasing (optional)

1 cup (7 oz/200 g) granulated sugar

Grated zest of 1 lemon

2 large eggs, at room temperature

½ cup (4 oz/115 g) sour cream

½ teaspoon pure vanilla extract

FOR THE LEMON GLAZE
¾ cup (3 oz/90 g) confectioners' sugar

3½ teaspoons fresh lemon juice

You can swap oranges for the lemons in this addictive citrus cake, or use a combination of both.

Wild Blueberry Crisp

A long-awaited summer fruit in Maine, wild blueberries taste absolutely amazing. And thanks to frozen wild blueberries, you can prepare this dessert year-round wherever you live. The crisp is versatile, so feel free to swap in other frozen or fresh berries; if they are very ripe and juicy, add another tablespoon of flour to the fruit mixture.

SERVES 6

Grease a 1½-qt (1.4-L) round ceramic baking dish with butter or coat with canola oil spray.

In a bowl, gently stir together the blueberries, granulated sugar, flour, and lemon juice. Transfer to the prepared baking dish.

To make the topping, in another bowl, stir together the oats, flour, brown sugar, oat bran, baking powder, cinnamon, ginger, and salt. Add the butter and rub into the flour mixture with your fingertips until the mixture is crumbly. Sprinkle evenly over the fruit.

Place the baking dish on the steam rack. Using the handles, lower the baking dish and the steam rack into the Instant Pot® and attach the air fryer lid. Press the Bake button and set the cook time for 30 minutes at 350°F (180°C), then press Start. Bake undisturbed.

When the cooking time is up, check to see if the crisp topping is golden and the fruit has started to bubble around the edges. If not, add more cooking time in 2-minute intervals until the crisp is cooked as desired. Using the steam rack handles, lift out the baking dish and transfer it to a wire rack until cool enough to handle. Use a large spoon to scoop heaping servings onto individual bowls. Serve warm with a scoop of vanilla ice cream alongside.

Unsalted butter, for greasing

3 cups (15 oz/425 g) frozen wild blueberries

3 tablespoons granulated sugar

1 tablespoon all-purpose flour

1 tablespoon fresh lemon juice

FOR THE TOPPING
⅔ cup (2½ oz/70 g) rolled oats (not quick cooking)

⅓ cup (1½ oz/40 g) all-purpose flour

⅓ cup (2¾ oz/80 g) firmly packed light brown sugar

¼ cup (¾ oz/20 g) oat bran

1 teaspoon baking powder

½ teaspoon ground cinnamon

½ teaspoon ground ginger

¼ teaspoon kosher salt

4 tablespoons (2 oz/60 g) cold unsalted butter, cut into small pieces

Vanilla ice cream, for serving

Giant Chocolate Chip Cookie

This confection combines the best of both worlds: a crispy skillet chocolate chip cookie and a tray of thick, gooey blondies. While the outside cooks up crunchy and golden, the inside stays melt-in-your-mouth soft. Bake it in a 7-inch (18-cm) round cake pan and cut into wedges to serve. Wrap slices individually for school lunches or special treats on the go.

SERVES 6

Grease a 7-inch (18-cm) round cake pan with butter and dust with flour. Alternatively, coat it with canola oil spray and dust with flour.

In a bowl, whisk together the flour, baking powder, and salt. Set aside.

In the bowl of a stand mixer fitted with the paddle attachment, beat together the butter and both sugars on medium-high speed until light and fluffy, 3–5 minutes. Add the eggs one at a time, beating well on medium speed after each addition. Add the vanilla and beat well until combined, about 1 minute. Add the flour mixture and beat on low speed until just combined, about 1 minute. Fold in the chocolate chips with a rubber spatula or wooden spoon. Pour the batter into the prepared pan. Sprinkle with flaky sea salt (if using).

Place the cake pan on the steam rack. Using the handles, lower the pan and the steam rack into the Instant Pot® and attach the air fryer lid. Press the Bake button and set the cook time for 20 minutes at 325°F (165°C), then press Start. Bake undisturbed.

When the cooking time is up, use a toothpick to check if the cookie is cooked all the way through; it should come out clean or with a few loose crumbs attached. If not, add more cooking time in 2-minute intervals until the cookie is light golden brown and cooked through. Using the steam rack handles, lift out the pan and transfer it to a wire rack until cool enough to handle. Remove the cookie from the pan by sliding a butter knife around the edges to loosen it. Place a plate on top of the pan, invert it, and shake gently to loosen the cookie onto the plate. Using a spatula, flip the cookie right-side-up onto the plate. Cut into wedges and serve.

1 cup (4 oz/115 g) all-purpose flour, plus more for dusting

1 teaspoon baking powder

½ teaspoon kosher salt

6 tablespoons (3 oz/90 g) unsalted butter, at room temperature, plus more for greasing (optional)

⅓ cup (2½ oz/70 g) granulated sugar

⅓ cup (2¾ oz/80 g) firmly packed light brown sugar

2 large eggs, at room temperature

1 teaspoon pure vanilla extract

1 cup (6 oz/170 g) semisweet chocolate chips

Flaky sea salt (optional)

Apple Fritters

The sweet, nutty, and creamy brown butter glaze that's poured over these hot apple goodies is hard to resist. A couple of tools will streamline the cooking process: a large, retractable ice cream scoop to shape the batter, plus air fryer liners or parchment paper to keep the fritters from sticking to the basket.

MAKES ABOUT 10

In a large bowl, whisk together the flour, baking powder, and salt. Stir in the milk with a rubber spatula or wooden spoon until just combined. In a medium bowl, toss together the apples, granulated sugar, and cinnamon until well coated. Fold the apples into the batter.

Line the Instant Pot® air fryer basket with an air fryer liner or parchment paper cut to fit. Working in batches, use a large ice cream scoop about 2 inches (5 cm) in diameter or a tablespoon measure to scoop equal-size portions of the batter, each about 3 tablespoons, onto the liner or parchment, spacing the fritters at least ½ inch (12 mm) apart. Coat the fritters with canola oil spray. Insert the basket into the pot and attach the air fryer lid. Press the Air Fry button and set the cook time for 12 minutes at 390°F (199°C), then press Start. Bake undisturbed.

Meanwhile, make the brown butter glaze: In a small saucepan over medium-high heat, melt the butter. Continue cooking the butter until it is light brown and starting to foam, swirling the pan occasionally. Watch the butter carefully at the end to prevent it from burning. Remove from the heat and let cool slightly. (There will be small, brown specks in the butter.) Place the confectioners' sugar in a small bowl or glass measuring cup. Add the melted butter, milk, and vanilla and whisk to combine. The glaze should be thick but pourable. If needed, add more milk 1 teaspoon at a time until it reaches the desired consistency. (Since it will be poured over the hot fritters, it will liquefy quickly.)

When the cooking time is up, use tongs to carefully transfer the fritters to a plate. Pour the glaze over the top to coat the fritters completely. Repeat to bake and glaze the remaining batches. Serve warm.

1¾ cups (7½ oz/210 g) all-purpose flour

1 tablespoon baking powder

½ teaspoon kosher salt

1¼ cups (300 ml) whole milk

2 cups (8 oz/225 g) peeled, cored, and diced sweet apples (about 2), such as Pink Lady, Honeycrisp, Braeburn, or Jonagold

2 tablespoons granulated sugar

¼ teaspoon ground cinnamon

FOR THE BROWN BUTTER GLAZE

4 tablespoons (2 oz/60 g) unsalted butter

1 cup (3½ oz/100 g) confectioners' sugar

2 tablespoons whole milk, plus more as needed

½ teaspoon pure vanilla extract

Mini Berry Hand Pies

Fresh blueberries are the ideal filling for these tiny treats since they're firm enough to hold up to intense heat but tender enough to cook quickly. Homemade pastry using your favorite recipe is a wonderful upgrade here, but store-bought refrigerated pie dough makes this a go-to dessert any night of the week.

MAKES 12 HAND PIES

Line a rimmed baking sheet with parchment paper. Dust a work surface with flour. Place 1 pie dough round on the work surface and use a 4½-inch (11.5-cm) round cutter to cut 4 circles out of the dough. (Alternatively, use a small, sharp knife to trace around the top of a glass and cut circles out of the dough.) Transfer the circles to the prepared baking sheet. Gather up the scraps and roll out the dough twice more, to cut out 2 more circles. Transfer to the baking sheet. Repeat to cut out circles from the remaining dough round.

In a medium bowl, stir together the blueberries, sugar, cornstarch, lemon juice, cinnamon, and salt.

Place 1 tablespoon of the berry mixture on the top half of each circle, leaving a ½-inch (12-mm) border at the top. Brush the top edge of the dough with some of the egg mixture. Gently fold the bottom half of the dough over the berries, tucking them inside. Press the top edge gently with your fingers to seal the dough into a half-moon shape. Use the tines of a fork to crimp (or seal) the edge closed. Repeat to fill the remaining circles. Refrigerate until the dough is cold and firm, 15–20 minutes.

Coat the Instant Pot® air fryer basket with canola oil spray. Working in batches, brush the hand pies on both sides with the egg mixture and sprinkle with sugar. Arrange a single layer of hand pies in the basket, making sure they don't touch. Insert the basket into the pot and attach the air fryer lid. Press the Air Fry button and set the cook time for 15 minutes at 350°F (180°C), then press Start. Bake undisturbed.

When the cooking time is up, use tongs to transfer the hand pies to a plate. Repeat to bake the remaining batches.

All-purpose flour, for dusting

2 store-bought refrigerated pie dough rounds (each about 7 oz/200 g and 11 inches/28 cm in diameter)

½ cups (7½ oz/210 g) fresh or thawed frozen blueberries

3 tablespoons sugar, plus more for sprinkling

2 tablespoons cornstarch

1 tablespoon fresh lemon juice

½ teaspoon ground cinnamon

Pinch of kosher salt

1 large egg beaten with 1 tablespoon cold water

Mini Chocolate-Filled Scones

These fluffy, chocolate-filled bites boast an almost biscuit-like texture that makes them quite addictive. Little hands can help make, shape, and fill the dough with chocolate chunks. Include a slice of banana inside, too, if you like.

MAKES ABOUT 12 SCONES

In a large bowl, whisk together the flour, baking powder, and salt. In a medium bowl, whisk together 1 egg and the sugar until thick and creamy. Whisk in the milk and melted butter until combined. Add the egg mixture to the flour mixture and mix with a rubber spatula until just blended.

Line a rimmed baking sheet with parchment paper and coat the parchment with canola oil spray. Use a tablespoon measure, a small ice cream scoop about 1½ inches (4 cm) in diameter, or a melon baller to scoop a rounded tablespoon of the dough, then press a piece of chocolate into the center. Shape the dough into a ball, enclosing the chocolate completely. Roll the ball in the palm of your hands until smooth. (The balls should be 1½–2 inches/ 4–5 cm in diameter.) Place the balls on the prepared baking sheet.

Coat the Instant Pot® air fryer basket with canola oil spray. In a small bowl, whisk together the remaining egg and the water. Working in batches, brush the top of the balls with some of the egg mixture and arrange a single layer of balls in the basket, making sure they don't touch. Insert the basket into the pot and attach the air fryer lid. Press the Air Fry button and set the cook time for 7 minutes at 350°F (180°C), then press Start. Bake undisturbed.

When the cooking time is up, use tongs or a non-metal spatula to carefully transfer the scones to a plate. Repeat to bake the remaining batches.

VARIATION

Mini Chocolate-Banana Filled Scones: *Cut 1 banana into thin slices and add a slice to the center of each dough ball along with the piece of chocolate. (It's okay if the banana bends a little when shaping the dough into balls.) Bake the scones as directed above.*

1¾ cups (7½ oz/210 g) all-purpose flour

2 teaspoons baking powder

½ teaspoon kosher salt

2 large eggs

⅓ cup (2½ oz/70 g) granulated sugar

⅓ cup (80 ml) whole milk

2 tablespoons unsalted butter, melted and cooled

2 oz (60 g) dark or milk chocolate, cut into 12 large chunks

1 teaspoon water

Banana Bread

Although banana bread isn't typically baked in a Bundt pan, the pan's open shape combined with the intense heat of air frying produces an unbelievably light and almost cake-like texture. Sour cream keeps the batter moist, but you can substitute plain whole-milk or Greek yogurt if you like.

SERVES 6

Grease an 8-inch (20-cm) Bundt pan with butter or coat with canola oil spray.

In a bowl, whisk together the flour, baking soda, and salt. Set aside.

In the bowl of a stand mixer fitted with the paddle attachment, beat together the butter and sugar on medium-high speed until light and fluffy, 3 to 5 minutes. Stop the mixer and scrape down the sides of the bowl with a rubber spatula. Add the eggs one at a time, beating well on medium speed after each addition. (The batter will form ribbons at this stage.) Stop the mixer and scrape down the sides of the bowl. Add the bananas, sour cream, and vanilla and beat until just combined, about 2 minutes. Add the flour mixture and beat on low speed until just combined, about 1 minute. Pour the batter into the prepared pan.

Place the Bundt pan on the steam rack. Using the handles, lower the pan and the steam rack into the Instant Pot® and attach the air fryer lid. Press the Bake button and set the cook time for 27 minutes at 325°F (165°C), then press Start. Bake undisturbed.

When the cooking time is up, use a toothpick to check if the bread is cooked all the way through; it should come out clean or with a few loose crumbs attached. If not, add more cooking time in 2-minute intervals until the bread is cooked through. Using the steam rack handles, lift out the pan and transfer it to a wire rack until cool enough to handle. Remove the bread from the pan and return it to the wire rack. Let cool completely, then cut into wedges and serve.

1 cup (4 oz/115 g) all-purpose flour

1 teaspoon baking soda

1 teaspoon kosher salt

6 tablespoons (3 oz/90 g) unsalted butter, at room temperature, plus more for greasing (optional)

⅔ cup (4¾ oz/140 g) sugar

2 large eggs

1 cup (8 oz/225 g) mashed very ripe bananas (2 large or 3 medium)

⅓ cup (2½ oz/70 g) sour cream

½ teaspoon pure vanilla extract

Dark Chocolate Fudge Brownies

Rich, fudgy brownies are a cinch to make in the air fryer. The ingredients come together quickly in one saucepan, then the batter is poured into a 7-inch (18-cm) cake pan (or any round, heatproof baking dish that fits in the pot) and bakes for less than 30 minutes. Cut the brownies into wedges and serve with a giant scoop of ice cream alongside.

SERVES 6

Grease a 7-inch (18-cm) round cake pan with butter and dust with flour. Alternatively, coat it with canola oil spray and dust with flour, or use baking spray.

In a large saucepan over low heat, combine the chocolate and butter and heat, stirring occasionally, until melted and smooth, about 5 minutes. Remove from the heat and let cool slightly, then whisk in the sugar, vanilla, and salt. Whisk in the eggs one at a time, mixing well after each addition, then continue to whisk until the chocolate mixture is velvety and smooth, about 2 minutes. Add the flour and whisk until just blended. Pour the batter into the prepared pan.

Place the cake pan on the steam rack. Using the handles, lower the pan and the steam rack into the Instant Pot® and attach the air fryer lid. Press the Bake button and set the cook time for 28 minutes at 325°F (165°C), then press Start. Bake undisturbed.

When the cooking time is up, use a toothpick to check if the brownies are cooked all the way through; it should come out clean or with a few loose crumbs attached. If not, add more cooking time in 2-minute intervals until the brownies are springy to the touch and cooked through. Using the steam rack handles, lift out the pan and transfer it to a wire rack until cool enough to handle. Cut into wedges and serve with ice cream alongside, if desired.

3 oz (90 g) unsweetened chocolate, chopped

6 tablespoons (3 oz/90 g) unsalted butter, plus more for greasing (optional)

1 cup (7 oz/200 g) sugar

½ teaspoon pure vanilla extract

¼ teaspoon kosher salt

2 large eggs

½ cup (2 oz/60 g) all-purpose flour, plus more for dusting

Ice cream, for serving (optional)

Cinnamon-Raisin Bread Pudding

Brioche or challah bread is the ideal base for this creamy pudding. You can swap out the raisins for 1 cup (5 oz/140 g) fresh berries when they are in season. Assemble the bread pudding and let it rest in the refrigerator overnight, then bake the next morning for a super-simple brunch.

SERVES 6

Coat a 1½-qt (1.4-L) round ceramic baking dish with canola oil spray.

In a bowl, whisk together the eggs, cream, milk, the ⅓ cup (2½ oz/70 g) sugar, vanilla, ½ teaspoon of the cinnamon, and the salt. Arrange a single layer of bread cubes in the prepared baking dish so they nestle snugly and scatter half of the raisins on top. Layer the remaining bread cubes on top and scatter the remaining raisins over the bread. Pour the egg mixture over the top and press lightly to help the bread absorb the liquid. Cover with aluminum foil and refrigerate for at least 1 hour or up to overnight.

Pour the water into the Instant Pot® and place the baking dish, still covered with foil, on the steam rack. Using the handles, lower the baking dish and the steam rack into the pot. Lock the pressure-cooking lid in place and turn the valve to Sealing. Press the Pressure Cook button and set the cook time for 30 minutes at high pressure, then press Start.

When the cooking time is up, press the Quick Release Button or turn the valve to Venting to quick-release the steam. Carefully remove the lid. Using the steam rack handles, lift out the baking dish and remove the foil. Drain the water from the pot. Press the Cancel button to reset the program.

In a small bowl, stir together the remaining 1 tablespoon sugar and ½ teaspoon cinnamon. Sprinkle the cinnamon sugar evenly over the bread pudding. Return the baking dish and the steam rack to the pot and attach the air fryer lid. Press the Air Fry button and set the cook time for 5 minutes at 400°F (200°C), then press Start. Bake undisturbed.

Using the steam rack handles, lift out the baking dish and transfer it to a wire rack. Spoon the pudding onto individual plates and serve warm.

3 large eggs

¾ cup (180 ml) heavy cream

¾ cup (180 ml) whole milk

⅓ cup (2½ oz/70 g) plus 1 tablespoon sugar

1½ teaspoons pure vanilla extract

1 teaspoon ground cinnamon

¼ teaspoon kosher salt

¾ lb (340 g) brioche or challah bread, cut into 2-inch (5-cm) cubes

¼ cup (1½ oz/40 g) raisins

2 cups (475 ml) water

Jam-Filled Brioche Doughnuts

Jelly doughnuts, a highly coveted treat among the assorted-doughnut box, get a makeover that turns them into an everyday treat. Allow time for the dough to rest overnight and then proof once more the next day. Homemade strawberry jam (page 139) is the perfect filling, but any flavor of homemade or store-bought jam will taste great in these pillowy doughnuts, which can double as sandwich buns (minus the jam).

SERVES 6

In a large bowl, stir together the yeast, water, and egg. In a medium bowl, whisk together the flour, sugar, salt, and lemon zest. Add the flour mixture to the yeast mixture and use your fingers or a bowl scraper to mix until combined; it will be messy and sticky. Transfer the mixture to a work surface and knead until it starts to come together and feel like dough, 5–8 minutes. (Alternatively, mix the dough in the bowl of a stand mixer fitted with the paddle attachment for 4 minutes.)

Add the room-temperature butter to the dough, 1 tablespoon at a time, kneading after each addition until incorporated. Continue to knead the dough until glossy, smooth, and very elastic when stretched, 5–8 minutes longer. (If using a stand mixer, mix for 5 minutes.) Return the dough to the bowl, cover with plastic wrap, and let the dough rise in a warm spot until doubled in size, about 1 hour. Knock back the dough (give it a good punch), cover the bowl again, and refrigerate overnight or up to 1 day.

Line a rimmed baking sheet with parchment paper. Divide the dough into 6 equal pieces. Working with 1 piece at a time, place it on a work surface. Make a claw shape with your hand and place your palm loosely on top of the dough, then move your fingers in a circular motion around the dough to gently shape into a smooth ball. Transfer to the prepared baking sheet. Repeat with the remaining pieces of dough. Cover the baking sheet with plastic wrap and let stand in a warm spot until the balls are slightly springy when gently poked with your finger, 45 minutes–1 hour.

1¼ teaspoons active dry yeast

3 tablespoons water

1 large egg, lightly beaten

1½ cups (6½ oz/185 g) bread flour

3 tablespoons sugar

1 teaspoon kosher salt

Grated zest of ½ lemon

4 tablespoons (2 oz/60 g) unsalted butter, cut into 4 pieces, at room temperature, plus 2 tablespoons unsalted butter, melted

1 cup (10 oz/285 g) Strawberry Jam (page 139 or store-bought)

Confectioners' sugar, for dusting

continued from page 117

Coat the Instant Pot® air fryer basket with canola oil spray. Working in batches, arrange a single layer of doughnuts in the basket (about 3), making sure they don't touch. Coat the top of the doughnuts with canola oil spray. Insert the basket into the pot and attach the air fryer lid. Press the Air Fry button and set the cook time for 5 minutes at 375°F (190°C), then press Start. Bake undisturbed.

When the cooking time is up, use tongs or a non-metal spatula to carefully transfer the doughnuts to a plate. Immediately brush the top of the doughnuts with some of the melted butter. Repeat to bake the remaining batches.

Use a small, sharp knife to poke a deep, wide hole on one side of each doughnut, being careful not to poke through the other side. Fit a large pastry bag with a round tip. Fill the bag with the jam, leaving at least 2 inches (5 cm) at the top of the bag unfilled, and twist the top of the bag closed. To fill the doughnuts, insert the tip of the pastry bag into the hole, and pipe the jam until it reaches the top of the hole. (Alternatively, use a small espresso spoon or a ½-teaspoon measure to fill the doughnuts with jam.) Dust the top of the doughnuts with confectioners' sugar and serve.

VARIATION

Brioche Sandwich Buns: *Prepare the dough as directed but divide it into 4 equal pieces instead of 6. Bake 2 doughnuts at a time for 7 minutes, brushing them with melted butter immediately after baking. Cut in half crosswise and use as buns for Crispy Fried Chicken Sandwiches (page 69), Southwestern Turkey Burgers with Corn Relish (page 78), or Cheese-Stuffed Beef Burgers (page 64). (You may need to double or triple the bun recipe depending on the number of servings.)*

Cinnamon-Sugar French Toast Sticks

Kids and kids-at-heart will love this awesome breakfast treat. Use an air fryer liner or parchment paper to keep the basket clean when cooking. Maple syrup is a natural for dipping, or slather the sticks with homemade strawberry jam (page 139).

SERVES 4

In a bowl, whisk together the half-and-half, egg, granulated sugar, vanilla, and cinnamon. Working with a few bread strips at a time, dip them into the mixture to coat all sides, then place on a plate.

Line the Instant Pot® air fryer basket with an air fryer liner or parchment paper cut to fit. Working in batches, arrange a single layer of French toast sticks in the basket, making sure they don't touch. Insert the basket into the pot and attach the air fryer lid. Press the Air Fry button and set the cook time for 8 minutes at 400°F (200°C), then press Start. Flip the strips when prompted.

When the cooking time is up, use tongs to carefully transfer the sticks to a plate. Repeat to cook the remaining batches. Dust with confectioners' sugar and serve with maple syrup alongside for dipping.

½ cup (120 ml) half-and-half

1 large egg

2 tablespoons granulated sugar

½ teaspoon pure vanilla extract

¼ teaspoon ground cinnamon

10–12 oz (285–340 g) challah bread, cut into strips 4 by 1 by ¾ inches (10 by 2.5 by 2 cm)

Confectioners' sugar, for dusting

Maple syrup, for serving

Fried Banana Egg Rolls

These dessert egg rolls are an amazing combo of sweet and crunchy. Look for egg roll wrappers in the refrigerated section of Asian markets or large grocery stores. Be sure to secure the banana tightly when wrapping so the filling doesn't ooze out during cooking.

SERVES 8

In a small bowl, stir together the brown sugar and sesame seeds. Cut each banana in half lengthwise, then cut each half in half crosswise.

Working with 1 wrapper at a time, position a wrapper in a diamond shape on a work surface. (cover the other wrappers with a damp cloth so they won't dry out). Place 1 banana piece, flat side down, horizontally on the lower third of the wrapper. Lightly brush the edges of the wrapper with some of the beaten egg. Sprinkle 2 teaspoons of the brown sugar mixture on top of the banana. Fold the bottom corner over the banana, encasing it. Fold in the left and right corners toward the center and roll the wrapper away from you into a tight cylinder. Brush the seam with the beaten egg and press the edges firmly to seal. Transfer to a plate. Repeat with the remaining wrappers and banana pieces.

Working in batches, brush the egg rolls generously with the sesame oil and arrange a single layer of rolls in the Instant Pot® air fryer basket, making sure they don't touch. Insert the basket into the pot and attach the air fryer lid. Press the Air Fry button and set the cook time for 9 minutes at 390°F (199°C), then press Start. Cook undisturbed.

When the cooking time is up, the egg rolls should be light golden brown and slightly darker golden brown on the ends. If a darker color is desired, cook for 2 minutes longer. Use tongs to carefully transfer the egg rolls to a plate. Repeat to cook the remaining batches. Dust the egg rolls with confectioners' sugar and serve.

¼ cup (2 oz/60 g) firmly packed light brown sugar

2 tablespoons toasted sesame seeds

2 bananas (just underripe)

8 egg roll wrappers

1 large egg, beaten

2 tablespoons toasted sesame oil

Confectioners' sugar, for dusting

Egg roll wrappers made with real eggs work best; the vegan alternatives don't cook as well in the air fryer.

Churros con Chocolate

The Spanish-style doughnuts known as churros take some arm muscle to prepare, along with a bit of trust that a few simple ingredients can be transformed into such light and airy sweets. The key to success is following the visual cues outlined below,

SERVES 12

In a medium bowl, whisk together the flour and salt. Set aside.

In a high-sided large saucepan over medium heat, combine the water and butter cubes. Heat, stirring occasionally, until the butter is melted. Raise the heat to high and bring to a boil, then remove from the heat. Add all of the flour mixture at once and beat vigorously with a wooden spoon for a few seconds until the mixture is smooth and pulls away from the sides of the pan to form a ball. Place the pan over low heat and stir until the mixture starts to stick to the pan and create a film on the bottom, 30 seconds–1 minute. Remove from the heat and let stand for 1 minute.

In a small bowl, whisk 1 of the eggs. Set aside. Add the remaining eggs one at a time to the saucepan, beating thoroughly with a wooden spoon after each addition. Make sure the dough returns to its original texture before adding the second egg. (When adding the eggs, at first the mixture will be a sloppy mess. But as you beat vigorously, it will gradually become sticky and form a film again and eventually return to a smooth ball.) Add the beaten egg a little at a time, using just enough to form a dough that is very shiny and slowly drops from the spoon.

Fit a large pastry bag with a star tip (see note). Fill the bag with the dough, leaving at least 2 inches (5 cm) at the top of the bag unfilled. Twist the top of the bag closed and place in a tall glass.

½ cup (2 oz/60 g) bread flour

Generous pinch of kosher salt

½ cup (120 ml) water

4 tablespoons (2 oz/60 g) unsalted butter, cut into cubes, plus 2 tablespoons unsalted butter, melted

3 large eggs

¼ lb (115 g) semisweet chocolate, chopped

¼ cup (1¾ oz/50 g) sugar

1½ teaspoons ground cinnamon

especially when vigorously beating the eggs into the dough until it becomes a silky, smooth ball. Dunking the cinnamon-sugar–coated churros into warm melted chocolate makes all the effort worthwhile.

Line the Instant Pot® air fryer basket with an air fryer liner or parchment paper cut to fit. Working in batches, pipe strips of dough about 5 inches (13 cm) long onto the liner or parchment, spacing them at least 1 inch (2.5 cm) apart. (Return the pastry bag to the glass between piping batches.) Coat the churros with canola oil spray. Insert the basket into the pot and attach the air fryer lid. Press the Air Fry button and set the cook time for 15 minutes at 375°F (190°C), then press Start. Flip the churros when prompted.

Meanwhile, in a small saucepan over low heat, melt the chocolate, stirring occasionally. Pour into a small bowl. In a medium bowl or on a plate, stir together the sugar and cinnamon. Set aside.

When the cooking time is up, use tongs to carefully transfer the churros to a plate. Brush on all sides with some of the melted butter and roll in the cinnamon sugar. Repeat to cook the remaining batches. Serve with the melted chocolate alongside for dipping. Churros are best eaten hot out of the air fryer. You can let the dough stand at room temperature for up to 1 hour, or refrigerate if letting it stand longer, while you enjoy the churros in batches.

NOTE *Churros are typically shaped using a pastry bag fitted with a star tip, but if you don't have one, transfer the dough to a large lock-top plastic bag. Cut about ½ inch (12 mm) off one corner of the bag to create an opening to pipe the dough. If you like, use the tines of a fork to make lengthwise ridges in the piped dough to replicate the traditional shape.*

Glazed Buttermilk Doughnuts

Choose your favorite glaze—or try all three—on these addictive doughnuts, which are best eaten fresh from the air fryer. The glaze should be thick since it will melt quickly on the hot doughnuts. Dip them in a bowl of glaze and swirl gently, or pour it on top using a glass measuring cup. Either way, don't forget the colorful sprinkles.

SERVES 10

To make the doughnuts, in a medium bowl, whisk together both flours, baking powder, baking soda, salt, and nutmeg. Set aside.

In the bowl of a stand mixer fitted with the paddle attachment, beat together the egg and granulated sugar on medium-low speed until creamy and pale in color, about 2 minutes. Add the buttermilk, melted butter, and vanilla and beat until blended, about 1 minute. Stop the mixer and scrape down the sides of the bowl with a rubber spatula. Add the flour mixture and beat on low speed just until a soft dough forms, about 30 seconds. Cover the bowl with plastic wrap and refrigerate until the dough is firm, at least 30 minutes or up to 1 hour.

Line a rimmed baking sheet with parchment paper. Turn the dough out onto a generously floured work surface and roll out into a 10-inch (25-cm) round about ½ inch (12 mm) thick. Use a 3-inch (7.5-cm) round doughnut cutter to cut out as many doughnuts as possible. Transfer the doughnuts and doughnut holes to the prepared baking sheet. Gather up the scraps, reroll the dough, and cut out more doughnuts. (The dough will be sticky, so sprinkle it with flour as needed.) You should have about 10 doughnuts.

Coat the Instant Pot® air fryer basket with canola oil spray. Working in batches, arrange a single layer of doughnuts in the basket, making sure they don't touch. Insert the basket into the pot and attach the air fryer lid. Press the Air Fry button and set the cook time for 5 minutes at 375°F (190°C), then press Start. Bake undisturbed.

FOR THE DOUGHNUTS

1¼ cups (5½ oz/155 g) all-purpose flour, plus more for dusting

1 cup (4 oz/115 g) cake flour

1 teaspoon baking powder

½ teaspoon baking soda

½ teaspoon kosher salt

¼ teaspoon ground nutmeg

1 large egg

½ cup (3½ oz/100 g) granulated sugar

½ cup (120 ml) buttermilk, preferably full-fat

1 tablespoon unsalted butter, melted and cooled slightly

1 teaspoon pure vanilla extract

continued from page 124

Meanwhile, prepare the glazes: To make the chocolate glaze, in a saucepan over medium heat, combine the cream, butter, and corn syrup. Cook, stirring occasionally, until the butter melts and the mixture is hot but not boiling, 2–3 minutes. Remove from the heat and add the chocolate but don't stir. Let stand for about 30 seconds, then stir until the chocolate is melted and the glaze is smooth. Stir in the vanilla. Let the glaze cool until thickened, about 15 minutes. Transfer the glaze to a bowl. To make the vanilla glaze, in a small bowl, stir together the confectioners' sugar, milk, and vanilla. To make the lemon glaze, in a small bowl, stir together the confectioners' sugar and lemon juice. Set the glazes aside.

Line another rimmed baking sheet with parchment paper.

When the cooking time is up, use tongs or a non-metal spatula to carefully transfer the doughnuts to the prepared baking sheet. Repeat to bake the remaining batches.

Working with 1 doughnut at a time, dip the top side in the desired glaze and swirl slightly to coat, letting any excess drip back into the bowl. Return the doughnut to the baking sheet and decorate with sprinkles, if desired.

FOR THE CHOCOLATE GLAZE

⅓ cup (80 ml) heavy cream

4 tablespoons (2 oz/60 g) unsalted butter, cut into cubes

3 tablespoons light corn syrup

¼ lb (115 g) semisweet chocolate, chopped

1 teaspoon pure vanilla extract

FOR THE VANILLA GLAZE

1 cup (3½ oz/100 g) confectioners' sugar

2 tablespoons whole milk

½ teaspoon pure vanilla extract

FOR THE LEMON GLAZE

1 cup (3½ oz/100 g) confectioners' sugar

2 tablespoons plus 2 teaspoons fresh lemon juice

Rainbow sprinkles, for decorating (optional)

BASICS

Homemade Stock

We can probably all agree that any dish made with homemade stock is better than those made with the store-bought version. While meat stocks used to require the better part of an afternoon to prepare, with this method you can shave hours off that time and eliminate the need to keep an eye on the stockpot. Store extra in the freezer to have on hand for quick weeknight meals.

MAKES ABOUT 3 QT (3 L)

CHICKEN STOCK

Season the chicken with the salt. Select Sauté on the Instant Pot®, press Start, and heat the oil. Working in batches, brown the chicken on both sides, about 3 minutes per side. Transfer to a plate as browned. Add the onion and carrots to the pot and cook, stirring occasionally, until browned, about 2 minutes. Add 1 cup (240 ml) of the water and bring to a simmer, stirring occasionally with a wooden spoon to scrape up any browned bits. Press the Cancel button to reset the program.

Return the chicken to the pot and add the garlic, parsley, thyme, bay leaves, peppercorns, and the remaining 11 cups (2.75 L) water, ensuring that the pot is no more than two-thirds full. Attach the pressure-cooking lid and turn the valve to Sealing. Press the Pressure Cook button and set the cook time for 60 minutes at high pressure, then press Start.

When the cooking time is up, let the steam release naturally, or for at least 20 minutes, then press the Quick Release Button or turn the valve to Venting to quick-release any residual steam. Carefully remove the lid and pour the stock through a fine-mesh sieve into a large bowl. Discard the solids. If desired, pour the stock into a fat separator to remove the fat (or chill the stock in the refrigerator until the fat solidifies on top, then remove it with a spoon). Let the stock cool completely, then ladle into airtight storage containers. Refrigerate for up to 4 days or freeze for up to 3 months

TIP *You can skip the browning step and put all of the raw ingredients into the pot instead, but keep in mind that the flavor will be milder..*

3 lb (1.4 kg) chicken parts (drumsticks, backs, necks, and wings)

2 teaspoons kosher salt

1 tablespoon olive oil

1 yellow onion, roughly chopped

2 carrots, cut into 3-inch (7.5-cm) pieces

12 cups (3 L) water

2 cloves garlic, smashed

3 fresh flat-leaf parsley sprigs

3 fresh thyme sprigs

2 bay leaves

¼ teaspoon whole black peppercorns

VEGETABLE STOCK

Combine all the ingredients in the Instant Pot®, ensuring when you add the water that the pot is no more than two-thirds full. Attach the pressure-cooking lid and turn the valve to Sealing. Press the Pressure Cook button and set the cook time for 30 minutes at high pressure, then press Start.

When the cooking time is up, let the steam release naturally, or for at least 20 minutes, then press the Quick Release Button or turn the valve to Venting to quick-release any residual steam. Carefully remove the lid and pour the stock through a fine-mesh sieve into a large bowl. Discard the solids. Let the stock cool completely, then ladle into airtight storage containers. Refrigerate for up to 4 days or freeze for up to 3 months.

2 yellow onions, roughly chopped

2 ribs celery, roughly chopped

2 carrots, roughly chopped

1 cup (90 g) white button or cremini mushrooms, roughly sliced

4 cloves garlic, smashed

4 fresh flat-leaf parsley sprigs

2 bay leaves

1 teaspoon whole black peppercorns

10 cups (2.5 L) water

BEEF STOCK

Combine all the ingredients in the Instant Pot®, ensuring when you add the water that the pot is no more than two-thirds full. Attach the pressure-cooking lid and turn the valve to Sealing. Press the Pressure Cook button and set the cook time for 2 hours at high pressure, then press Start.

When the cooking time is up, let the steam release naturally, or for at least 20 minutes, then press the Quick Release Button or turn the valve to Venting to quick-release any residual steam. Carefully remove the lid and pour the stock through a fine-mesh sieve into a large bowl. Discard the solids. If desired, pour the stock into a fat separator to remove the fat (or chill the stock in the refrigerator until the fat solidifies on top, then remove it with a spoon). Let the stock cool completely, then ladle into airtight storage containers. Refrigerate for up to 4 days or freeze for up to 3 months.

3 lb (1.4 kg) beef marrow bones, cracked by a butcher

2 thick slices (about 1 lb/ 450 g) meaty beef shin

2 carrots, roughly chopped

2 ribs celery, roughly chopped

1 large yellow onion, roughly chopped

4 fresh flat-leaf parsley sprigs

1 bay leaf

½ teaspoon whole black peppercorns

8 cups (2 L) water

VARIATION

Bone Broth: *Roast the beef bones for 30–40 minutes in a preheated 450°F (230°C) oven. Add 1–2 tablespoons apple cider vinegar to the pot with the other ingredients and cook at high pressure for 3 hours. Release the steam naturally. (The bone broth has cooked long enough if the bones crumble when touched and the tendons, cartilage, and connective tissue have dissolved.) Strain and store the broth as directed above.*

HUMMUS

Combine the chickpeas, water, oil, and 1 teaspoon salt in the Instant Pot®. Attach the pressure-cooking lid and turn the valve to Sealing. Press the Pressure Cook button and set the cook time for 40 minutes at high pressure, then press Start.

When the cooking time is up, let the steam release naturally, or for at least 15 minutes, then press the Quick Release Button or turn the valve to Venting to quick-release any residual steam. Carefully remove the lid. Ladle 1 cup (240 ml) of the cooking liquid into a measuring cup. Drain the chickpeas in a colander set in the sink. Transfer the chickpeas to a blender or food processor. Add the garlic, lemon juice, tahini, cumin, 1 teaspoon of the paprika, 1 teaspoon salt, and ½ cup (120 ml) of the reserved cooking liquid. Blend until almost smooth, adding more cooking liquid and scraping down the sides of the blender as needed. With the blender running, add the oil through the pour spout in a slow, steady stream until incorporated, about 2 minutes. Taste and adjust the seasoning with salt.

Transfer the hummus to a serving bowl, sprinkle with the remaining paprika and red pepper flakes (if using), and drizzle with oil. Serve with pita chips and/or crudités.

1 cup (200 g) dried chickpeas, rinsed and picked over

4 cups (1 L) water

1 teaspoon canola oil

Kosher salt

2 cloves garlic, chopped

Juice of 1 lemon

¼ cup (60 g) tahini

¼ teaspoon ground cumin

2 teaspoons smoked paprika

¼ cup (60 ml) olive oil, plus more for serving

Red pepper flakes, for serving (optional)

FOR SERVING (OPTIONAL)
Pita chips (recipe follows) and/or crudités such as cauliflower florets, radishes, bell peppers, carrots, cucumber, and cherry tomatoes

PITA CHIPS

Brush the pita halves on both sides with the oil and sprinkle lightly with salt. Cut each half into 8 wedges.

Working in batches, arrange a single layer of pita wedges in the Instant Pot® air fryer basket, making sure they don't touch. Insert the basket into the pot and attach the air fryer lid. Press the Air Fry button and set the cook time for 10 minutes at 350°F (180°C), then press Start. Turn the chips when prompted.

When the cooking time is up, the wedges should be crisp and golden. If not, add more cooking time in 2-minute intervals until the wedges are cooked to the desired crispness. Use tongs to carefully transfer the pita chips to a plate. Repeat to cook the remaining batches.

4 pita breads, split in half horizontally along the seam

¼ cup (60 ml) olive oil

Kosher salt

Beans

Although canned beans are very convenient, they just don't taste the same as the home-cooked kind. Last-minute cooks, rejoice! The absolute best part about preparing beans this way is that they don't need to be soaked ahead of time. For bigger batches, double the quantities of beans, water, and oil.

MAKES ABOUT 3 CUPS (540 G)

BASIC BEANS

Combine the beans, water, oil, and salt to taste in the Instant Pot®. Attach the pressure-cooking lid and turn the valve to Sealing. Press the Beans/Chili button (or the Pressure Cook button) and set the cook time for the cooking time designated in the chart below at high pressure, then press Start.

When the cooking time is up, let the steam release naturally, or for at least 15 minutes, then press the Quick Release Button or turn the valve to Venting to quick-release any residual steam. Carefully remove the lid and drain the beans in a colander set in the sink.

TIP If you would prefer to soak your beans, soak 1 cup (200 g) beans in 4 cups (1 L) water for at least 4 hours or up to 12 hours, then cook them in their soaking water. They will cook in about half the time needed for unsoaked beans.

1 cup (200 g) dried beans, chickpeas, or lentils, rinsed and picked over

4 cups (1 L) water

1 teaspoon canola oil

1-2 teaspoons kosher salt

COOKING TIMES FOR UNSOAKED BEANS & LENTILS

Green, Brown, or Black Lentils	15 minutes
Black Beans	20-25 minutes
Navy Beans	20-25 minutes
Pinto Beans	20-25 minutes
Cannellini Beans	35-40 minutes
Chickpeas	35-40 minutes

Mozzarella Sticks with
Marinara Sauce (page 25)

MAKES 2½ CUPS (625 G)

POLENTA

Select Sauté on the Instant Pot® and press Start. Add the liquid and 2 teaspoons salt and bring to a boil. Slowly stream in the polenta, whisking constantly to prevent clumping. Press the Cancel button to reset the program.

Attach the pressure-cooking lid and turn the valve to Sealing. Press the Pressure Cook button and set the cook time for 8 minutes at high pressure, then press Start.

When the cooking time is up, press the Quick Release Button or turn the valve to Venting to quick-release the steam. Carefully remove the lid. Season the polenta to taste with salt and pepper. Stir in the butter and cheese (if using) and serve.

4 cups (1 L) liquid, such as water, whole milk, and/or chicken stock (page 130 or store-bought)

Kosher salt and freshly ground black pepper

1 cup (160 g) polenta

2 tablespoons unsalted butter (optional)

½ cup (60 g) freshly grated Parmesan cheese (optional)

MAKES 4 CUPS (950 ML)

MARINARA SAUCE

Combine the stock, tomatoes, tomato paste, oil, mustard, basil, oregano, red pepper flakes, ½ teaspoon salt, and ½ teaspoon black pepper in the Instant Pot® and whisk to blend. Attach the pressure-cooking lid and turn the valve to Sealing. Press the Pressure Cook button and set the cook time for 5 minutes at high pressure, then press Start.

When the cooking time is up, let the steam release naturally for 5 minutes, then press the Quick Release Button or turn the valve to Venting to quick-release any residual steam. Carefully remove the lid. Stir, then taste and adjust the seasoning with salt and black pepper. The sauce can be stored in an airtight container in the refrigerator for up to 5 days.

2 cups (475 ml) chicken or vegetable stock (page 130–131 or store-bought)

1 can (28 oz/800 g) crushed tomatoes

½ cup (4 oz/115 g) tomato paste

¼ cup (60 ml) olive oil

1 tablespoon Dijon mustard

1 tablespoon chopped fresh basil

2 teaspoons dried oregano

1 teaspoon red pepper flakes, plus more if desired

Kosher salt and freshly ground black pepper

Rice

Cooking rice can be a daunting task, not to mention a long one, when it comes to brown and wild rice varieties. This method is quick and can be easily adjusted for your texture preference. If you like softer rice, add ¼ cup (60 ml) more water to the pot at the beginning, or let the steam release naturally for a longer period of time.

MAKES ABOUT 4 CUPS (640 G)

WHITE RICE

Combine the rice, water, and salt in the Instant Pot®. Attach the pressure-cooking lid and turn the valve to Sealing. Press the Pressure Cook button and set the cook time for 4 minutes at high pressure, then press Start.

When the cooking time is up, let the steam release naturally for 10 minutes, then press the Quick Release Button or turn the valve to Venting to quick-release any residual steam. Carefully remove the lid and fluff the rice with a fork. If the rice feels too moist, place a kitchen towel over the pot and let the steam evaporate for a few minutes longer, until your desired texture is reached.

2 cups (400 g) long-grain white rice, such as jasmine or basmati, rinsed well and drained

2 cups (475 ml) water

½ teaspoon kosher salt

MAKES ABOUT 4 CUPS (800 G)

BROWN RICE

Combine the rice, water, and salt in the Instant Pot®. Attach the pressure-cooking lid and turn the valve to Sealing. Press the Pressure Cook button and set the cook time for 15 minutes at high pressure, then press Start.

When the cooking time is up, let the steam release naturally for 10 minutes, then press the Quick Release Button or turn the valve to Venting to quick-release any residual steam. Carefully remove the lid and fluff the rice with a fork. If the rice feels too moist, place a kitchen towel over the pot and let the steam evaporate for a few minutes longer, until your desired texture is reached.

2 cups (370 g) long-grain brown rice

2½ cups (600 ml) water

½ teaspoon kosher salt

COCONUT RICE

Combine the rice, coconut milk, water, sugar, and salt in the Instant Pot®. Attach the pressure-cooking lid and turn the valve to Sealing. Press the Pressure Cook button and set the cook time for 4 minutes at high pressure, then press Start.

When the cooking time is up, let the steam release naturally for 10 minutes, then press the Quick Release Button or turn the valve to Venting to quick-release any residual steam. Carefully remove the lid and fluff the rice with a fork. If the rice feels too moist, place a kitchen towel over the pot and let the steam evaporate for a few minutes longer, until your desired texture is reached. Serve with toppings, if desired.

2 cups (400 g) long-grain white rice, such as jasmine or basmati, rinsed well and drained

1 can (13.5 oz/400 ml) full-fat coconut milk

½ cup (120 ml) water

½ teaspoon sugar

½ teaspoon kosher salt

FOR SERVING (OPTIONAL)
Toasted shredded coconut, chopped green onions, lime wedges

WILD RICE

Combine the rice, water, and salt in the Instant Pot®. Attach the pressure-cooking lid and turn the valve to Sealing. Press the Pressure Cook button and set the cook time for 30 minutes at high pressure, then press Start.

When the cooking time is up, let the steam release naturally for 10 minutes, then press the Quick Release Button or turn the valve to Venting to quick-release any residual steam. Carefully remove the lid and fluff the rice with a fork. If the rice feels too moist, place a kitchen towel over the pot and let the steam evaporate for a few minutes longer, until your desired texture is reached.

2 cups (400 g) long-grain white rice, such as jasmine or basmati

2 cups (475 ml) water

½ teaspoon kosher salt

QUINOA

Combine the quinoa, water, and salt in the Instant Pot®. Attach the pressure-cooking lid and turn the valve to Sealing. Press the Pressure Cook button and set the cook time for 1 minute at high pressure, then press Start.

When the cooking time is up, let the steam release naturally for 10 minutes, then press the Quick Release Button or turn the valve to Venting to quick-release any residual steam. Carefully remove the lid and fluff the quinoa with a fork.

1 cup (180 g) quinoa (red, white, or mixed), rinsed

1¼ cups (300 ml) water

½ teaspoon kosher salt

FARRO

Combine the farro, water, and salt in the Instant Pot®. Attach the pressure-cooking lid and turn the valve to Sealing. Press the Pressure Cook button and set the cook time for 10 minutes at high pressure, then press Start.

When the cooking time is up, let the steam release naturally for 10 minutes, then press the Quick Release Button or turn the valve to Venting to quick-release any residual steam.

1 cup (210 g) farro

1 cup (240 ml) water

½ teaspoon kosher salt

PEARL BARLEY

Combine the barley, water, and salt in the Instant Pot®. Attach the pressure-cooking lid and turn the valve to Sealing. Press the Pressure Cook button and set the cook time for 20 minutes at high pressure for a chewier texture and up to 22 minutes for a soft texture, then press Start.

When the cooking time is up, let the steam release naturally for 10 minutes, then press the Quick Release Button or turn the valve to Venting to quick-release any residual steam.

1 cup (200 g) pearl barley

2½ cups (600 ml) water

½ teaspoon kosher salt

STRAWBERRY JAM

Sterilize your jam jars (see note below).

Press the Sauté button on the Instant Pot®, add the honey, then press Start. Cook until the honey is soft enough to stir (cook time will vary depending on whether you use regular or raw honey). Add the strawberries, bring to a boil, and cook, stirring occasionally, for about 3 minutes until the strawberries start to soften. Press the Cancel button to reset the program.

Attach the pressure-cooking lid and turn the valve to Sealing. Press the Pressure Cook button and set the cook time for 3 minutes at high pressure, then press Start.

When the cooking time is up, let the steam release naturally, or for at least 15 minutes, then press the Quick Release Button or turn the valve to Venting to quick-release any residual steam. Carefully remove the lid. Use a fork to mash the strawberries, or blend until smooth (or still somewhat chunky, if desired) either by transferring the mixture to a stand blender or using an immersion blender in the pot. If you used a stand blender, return the jam to the pot. Press the Sauté button, press Start, and simmer to reduce any excess liquid, stirring occasionally, until the jam is thick enough to coat the back of a spoon, about 5 minutes.

Transfer the jam to the sterilized jam jars (using a heatproof jam funnel will help) and let cool completely, uncovered, at room temperature. Once the jam is cooled, cover and store in the refrigerator for up to 2 weeks.

¾ cup (250 g) regular honey or raw honey

1 lb (450 g) strawberries, hulled and sliced

NOTE *If your Instant Pot® model has a Sterilize button, you can sterilize your jam jars in the pot. Place the steam rack inside the pot and add 2 cups (475 ml) water. Place two 8-oz (240-ml) jam jars on top of the steam rack. Attach the pressure-cooking lid and turn the valve to Sealing. Press the Sterilize button at the normal setting. When the cooking time is up, press the Quick Release Button or turn the valve to Venting to quick-release the steam, remove the lid, and, using tongs or oven mitts, carefully transfer the jam jars to a plate or cutting board. Cover with a dish towel to keep them warm. Discard the water.*

If your Instant Pot® does not have a Sterilize button, you can run jam jars through the hottest setting of your dishwasher or boil them in a large pot of water.

INDEX

AIR FRYING WITH INSTANT POT®

Conceived and produced by Weldon Owen International
in collaboration with Williams Sonoma, Inc.
3250 Van Ness Avenue, San Francisco, CA 94109

A WELDON OWEN PRODUCTION

1150 Brickyard Cove Road
Richmond, CA 94801
www.weldonowen.com

Printed in China
10 9 8 7 6 5 4 3 2 1

Library of Congress
Cataloging-in-Publication data is available.

ISBN: 978-1-68188-605-3

WELDON OWEN INTERNATIONAL

CEO Raoul Goff
Publisher Roger Shaw
Associate Publisher Amy Marr
Editorial Assistant Jourdan Plautz
Creative Director Chrissy Kwasnik
Designer Megan Sinead Harris

Managing Editor Lauren LePera
Production Manager Binh Au
Imaging Manager Don Hill

Photographer Erin Scott
Food Stylist Lillian Kang
Prop Stylist Claire Mack

Weldon Owen wishes to thank the following people
for their generous support in producing this book:
Kris Balloun, Lesley Bruynesteyn, and Elizabeth Parson.